I Never Signed

Up For This...

Finding Power in Life's Broken Pieces

Darryle Pollack

for Alli, Daniel and V

Putting together the broken pieces in the mosaic of my life,

your love fills in all the empty spaces

Table of Contents:

Introduction

I never signed up for this...I think I've earned the right to this title since I've said those words so many times.

Maybe you have, too.

I expected life to unfold just like the fairy tales we read as kids. And just as it was supposed to, my path rolled out perfectly—innocent childhood, intact family, safe community—plus a few bonus scenarios like an Ivy League education, a magical exciting career and a movie star responsible for my marriage. I took all of that in stride, as if I expected it. Which maybe I did.

But what about those things I *didn't* expect? Bumps. Barriers. Blows. Breakage. Stuff that isn't supposed to happen does happen to all of us. Whether you lose the wedding ring or the husband who gave it to you, no one gets through life without experiencing loss, pain, and challenges. At some point, many of us look around and wonder how we got there.

I never signed up for this...

...it's a more polite and palatable way to say *WTF* or *Shit Happens.* I just didn't think those would be very good book titles.

We embark on our lives without any ability to predict what's ahead. We should expect the unexpected. Given today's world, it's a given that everyone will experience change, challenge, and crisis. That magnifies the importance of our ability to adapt, the ability that has allowed us to survive and thrive as a species. Our

1

capacity to adapt has never been more essential than it is today when change happens at warp speed.

Those times when we say *"I never signed up for this…"* are the hinges that shift the story of every life.

The test of our characters, and our futures, depend on what we do AFTER we say *I never signed up for this.* Successful survival results from resilience, how we adapt to what happens. I'm not the first person to use the phrase *what breaks you can make you,* but I'm an example of why it's true.

As a young mom, I was forced to face my greatest fear. Naturally I said *"I never signed up for this…"* plus some other words I won't repeat. I never imagined that confronting what I most feared would ultimately determine and define who I am. What I learned helped me find the resilience to recreate my life, and hopefully provide insights that can help with yours.

My revelation started by surprise at the end of a yearlong nightmare of cancer treatment. Looking for a fun way to spend a few hours with my 7 year old son, I walked into a little pottery studio to paint a knick-knack. I was as far as you could get from artistic, and thought of myself as the anti-Martha Stewart. Yet those few hours, which started as a minor distraction, became a major lifeline. My crude artwork on that knick-knack developed into a passion for painting ceramics and creating mosaics out of broken pieces of tile.

Then came my epiphany: suddenly I could see, in a very concrete literal way, what resilience looks like. What I was doing with those broken pieces of tile was exactly what I was doing with the broken pieces of my life. I was picking up the pieces and putting them together to make something different from what I started with.

Mosaics are a metaphor for life.

This simple art process profoundly transformed my mindset. Discovering the power in those broken pieces was a powerful demonstration proving to me that *what breaks you can make you.*

We take our broken pieces: our broken families, broken hearts, broken dreams. We pick them up and we rearrange them into something new. Just like a mosaic, an assemblage of broken life pieces can be put together to make something new that is beautiful in a different way.

I arranged this book around my biggest broken pieces, because putting them together in a new way made me grow, made me strong, made me the artist of my own life. I found power in life's broken pieces and I hope that reading this book will inspire you to do the same.

The First Break

Miami Beach was such a beautiful place to grow up, sometimes I met people who didn't believe ordinary folks lived in such a glamorous setting. Surrounded by sparkling ocean and stately palm trees, our peaceful piece of paradise was a close-knit community where I went to public school with the same kids from pre-school to high school. We rode bikes down the busiest boulevards, took city busses everywhere, strolled on Lincoln Road before it was turned into a pedestrian mall, and went to the public beaches on Collins Avenue before the canyons of condos hid the ocean from view.

Most Miami Beach kids were like me and lived in a house on a safe street with both parents. Like the other moms I knew, my mom didn't work, other than her very active involvement with United Cerebral Palsy. Mom was younger and more elegant and prettier than everyone else's mom. At least I thought so. Even her name was beautiful: Marcella Tartell. Given her background growing up in Brooklyn with a divorced mother, I'm not sure where or how she acquired the class she exuded. Glamorous, gracious, and gentle, she was admired by the other parents; appreciated by the other kids. Despite her movie star beauty, she was just as beautiful inside. Kind and warm, serene and calm; at the same time she was lively, fun, and full of life.

Taken around 1950, after she had a baby and graduated from college,
my mom looked like a movie star posing by a hotel pool in Miami Beach.

Mom, in her Lana-Turner-look-a-like phase,
with me and my sister Carla, in 1953.

Even as a teenager, I didn't rebel. I felt proud and lucky to be her daughter. I can't think of a single complaint I ever had about my Mom. Except maybe that she passed on a gene for a serious addiction—to chocolate.

On the other hand, I had a long list of complaints about my dad. I could hardly believe there were daughters who had their daddies wrapped around their little fingers. Mine was a tough businessman who meant business as a parent, too. A male version of a Tiger Mother, Tiger Dad laid down strict rules and expected

them to be followed. He set high expectations and expected them to be met. To college admissions officers, a couple C's on my report card sophomore year was a blemish on my high school record. To my father, this was a disaster, requiring drastic measures—for an entire semester I was forbidden to date, go out on weekends, or even use the phone.

Taken around 1950, either just before or soon after my parents *became* parents.

In other ways Dad was unexpectedly easier to please. The first time I made homemade brownies, I cried when they came out of the oven burnt to a crisp. Dad went crazy for them. He told me I took after his mother, who could speak seven languages but was hopeless at translating a recipe.

This softer side wasn't exposed often. My father's fixation on my childhood chubbiness tormented me. At a restaurant, Dad would stop a waiter with serving spoon in mid-air, about to deposit mashed potatoes onto my plate. "Just give her the vegetables," he'd announce. Mortified doesn't begin to describe it.

I stewed over his harshness but didn't have the guts or gumption to stand up to him, relying on someone else to fight my battles: either Mom or my 18-months-younger sister Carla. I was afraid of him. She wasn't.

Though he could be controlling and critical, I felt loved and adored. Dad thought I was smart. He thought I was pretty. It took maturity to realize

The family: Mom and Dad, me, Carla and Josh, around 1958 outside our home.

he could be both my toughest critic and my biggest fan.

By high school graduation and the approach of college, I had slimmed down. This relieved the pressure from Dad and was great timing for a major shopping expedition with Mom. I was starting Cornell in the fall, and my Miami Beach wardrobe wasn't going to cut it in Ithaca's frigid climate.

Mom loved clothes and fashion. Any chance to go shopping with her was a treat, especially in Manhattan, where Mom often shopped with her fashionista friend Lenore. A buyer for boutiques in the Midwest, Lenore provided access into wholesale houses in the Fashion District. What a thrill to be in such a sophisticated glamorous environment. And what a way to pick out my college wardrobe.

We'd enter a manufacturer's showroom (none of which I had ever heard of) and look at the fall collection. Lenore would pick out a skirt or sweater, and I'd try on the sample. If my mom and Lenore liked it, Mom would order it, sometimes in multiple colors, to be shipped to my college dorm. It was such a heady experience that I went along and said I liked everything, whether I did or not.

I acquired a wardrobe that would have been more appropriate for a suburban matron in Westchester than a college freshman in Ithaca. A collection of lady-like knit dresses. Thigh high patent leather boots. A camel-colored suit with a wide lambs' wool collar. A Dr. Zhivago—inspired coat with fur trim. Even with a busy social life, some of those clothes I never even wore once. Once I got to Cornell, I lived in jeans and t-shirts like everyone else.

The clothes were ultimately given away and forgotten, but not the shopping trip. Over the decades, it's remained memorable for many reasons: having time alone with my mom;

feeling grown up; the anticipation of entering a new phase of life. Most of all, I remember this college shopping trip as a magical fantasy that existed on the other side of a door that suddenly slammed shut in my face, leaving a permanent fault line in the foundation of my well-being.

When I flew home from Cornell for spring break freshman year, there was a surprise waiting for me at the Miami airport. Neal Walk had been the center and the star of Beach High's state championship basketball team when I was a sophomore. He would go on to play professional basketball for the New York Knicks and Phoenix Suns. We had met and dated the summer before I went to college when we were both camp counselors, and we had stayed in touch. Neal was 6'll" and it was impossible to miss him at the airport, but I did miss the significance that he came to meet me instead of my parents.

Mom was in bed when I got home, looking tired and wearing a pink quilted bed jacket. Had I been more tuned in, I might have seen this as an indicator of something unsettling. I didn't notice.

I did notice a month later, when my mother entered the hospital for a "back problem." In those days, without cell phones, internet, and instant contact, this news was communicated by my dad in the usual way—a weekly phone conversation held over the hall phone in my dorm. Dad and I hatched a plan for me to fly down the next week and surprise Mom in the hospital on Mother's Day.

My trip started the day before Mother's Day, six bumpy hours from Ithaca to Manhattan in my boyfriend's old rickety red and white VW bus. The next morning I switched gears and joined the jet set. Carrying just a purse and no luggage, I caught a flight to Miami, eager to be my mother's special delivery surprise gift. I picked out a special outfit: brown cotton culottes with a beige top and matching floppy hat. The most memorable and important feature of this outfit was that I tucked the top into the waist of the culottes, significant because I had recently lost weight and hoped my critical father might notice.

Arriving in Miami, I took a taxi directly from the airport to Jackson Memorial Hospital. Had I bothered to consider the oddity of this, it might have lit a warning light in my brain. We lived just a few blocks from Mount Sinai, the hospital of choice for pretty much anything if you lived on Miami Beach. By contrast, Jackson Memorial was in downtown Miami, an inner city, no-frills teaching hospital affiliated with the University of Miami Medical School. At the time I never knew anyone who had ever been there.

That didn't cross my mind as I jumped out of my cab and exuberantly bounced upstairs, ready to spring into my mother's hospital room as her surprise gift in my cute little outfit and hat.

The wind was sucked out of my sails the minute I walked into the room and took in the scene. Mom was surprised; she even cried. She was happy to see me and my father brought flowers, but there was absolutely nothing festive about the atmosphere in that room. It was medicinal. Plus Mom actually looked *sick*—not like a 41 year old healthy woman who was having a little back trouble and would soon be back to normal. She seemed weak, almost frail.

I had no idea—and no one told me—that this is how a person looks who is dying of cancer.

That day is so clear in my memory that I have a hard time trying to comprehend how I completely missed the reality. At 18, I thought of myself as sophisticated and independent—I had visited prospective colleges and moved into my freshman dorm on my own. Underneath, maybe I was just young and naïve. Maybe I was too wrapped up in myself and my life at school. Maybe I was in deep denial because I was scared. Maybe all of those.

Completely oblivious, I spent those few hours casually chatting about my boyfriend David and my friends back at school. Then I flew back to Ithaca. I didn't forget about my mom, far away in that bare hospital room, but I wasn't overly worried either. Those were the days before insurance companies set time limits on hospital stays. It didn't occur to me to question my dad when he continued to tell me Mom was still in the hospital.

Freshman year ended two weeks later. I went ahead with my plans to visit friends in various cities on the East Coast. After only a few days, Dad summoned me home from Boston because Mom was having a "back operation." I adored my mother, but I also remember feeling a little annoyed that my trip was cut short.

I spent the month of June at home with my father, my sister Carla, and my younger brother Josh, while Mom remained in the hospital. Every day I drove from Miami Beach to Jackson Memorial to see her for a few hours. But I also spent that month doing normal things—seeing friends, going to the beach and to movies, preparing to leave for my summer job as a camp counselor.

Over the years since June 1968 I've looked back on that month—the friends I haven't kept, the movies I don't remember. If I'd had any inkling that it would be the last month of my mother's life, I would have spent it at her bedside, inhaling her wisdom, her memories, her advice, her serenity, her love. The loss of that precious time and knowledge left a crater in my life that is unfixable.

People have asked me, and I've wondered myself, what I thought was going on. My mother had been in the hospital for weeks. She looked terrible. I was a smart kid. Couldn't I figure it out?

There were plenty of clues, if I had only wanted to look. Maybe I just didn't want to see.

Back then, no one talked about cancer. Having cancer was a secret, a stigma, almost shameful. Any mention of the word itself came in a voice dropped to a barely audible whisper. "He has...cancer." It never occurred to me that Mom had it, or anything serious.

Mystified by science and medicine, I accepted the explanations I was given: "back trouble" and "complications" from being hospitalized. Although I was already 18, you didn't question adults, certainly not doctors. Plus, of course I wanted and needed to believe this was just a medical glitch. Pretty soon Mom would be home, back to her usual self.

My grandmother, my mother's mother, lived in Miami, and Mom also had one sister who lived in New York. But the person who was there at the hospital every day with Mom was her friend Helen. She wasn't my real aunt, but we called her Aunt Helen, as her kids called my mother "Aunt Marcy."

Normally we hardly ever saw Aunt Helen. She was older and very different from my mom, but she was Mom's closest confidante. Not until decades later did I have an appreciation of that friendship, and what women's friendships could mean. I realize now that Aunt Helen must have heard whatever deep fears and pain my mother might have been able to express.

Aunt Helen was the only adult I knew who didn't drive. Her husband Ben must have driven her from their home every day to Jackson Memorial, over an hour away. I have no idea who was taking care of her own children, but Aunt Helen was there when I got to the hospital every single day, tending to my mother, putting on her makeup, fixing up her hair, talking to her, laughing with her.

On the day Bobby Kennedy died, Aunt Helen intercepted me in the hallway. "Don't tell your mother. She loves Bobby so much. I don't want her to be sad." As it turned out, a nurse told Mom about Bobby Kennedy. It didn't occur to me why Aunt Helen would be so worried about my mother's state of mind if she only had "back trouble."

As the oldest child, I offered to stay home for the summer while Mom was still in the hospital. Both my parents said absolutely not, there was no reason for that, and pressed me to go ahead with my plan to be a counselor again at Camp Anawana in Monticello, New York, where my brother Josh would be a camper. So one day at the end of June, Josh and I stopped by the hospital to say goodbye to Mom, then flew to New York.

After a few days enjoying Manhattan, we showed up on a Sunday morning to meet the chartered camp bus at a public school parking lot crowded with parents and kids. I had been a counselor the summer before, and was excited to go back. Searching for my girls, I ran into Mel, the waterfront counselor, who I knew well from the previous summer. Mel was on his way to his car and offered to relieve me of the garment bag I was carrying and take it up to camp. It was heavy and bulky, and contained all my dressy clothes. I was glad to hand it over.

Josh found his group, I found mine. We boarded our separate buses surrounded by excited kids saying goodbye to parents for 8 weeks. I greeted people from the previous summer and noticed all the new faces. Then I noticed another face, totally out of context, boarding our bus just before it was due to roll out of Manhattan. It was my aunt Lydia, the wife of my father's brother. She lived in Queens, and we hardly ever saw her. It was completely weird for her to be there. I started to get a funny feeling in my stomach.

Aunt Lydia was suddenly taking charge of us. "Your dad decided he didn't want you in camp after all. He thought it would be better for you to be home. He booked a flight and he sent me here to get you both to the airport. I already told the camp director you're going home."

Josh and I were too confused and apprehensive to protest. Besides, you didn't argue with my father. Even in absentia.

Just like that, we were gone. On the way to Aunt Lydia's car I remembered Mel, who was probably already on the George Washington Bridge with my garment bag.

In strained solemn silence, 13-year-old Josh and I sat together in Lydia's car from Manhattan to LaGuardia, and then on the plane to Miami. I might have tried to comfort him, and I should have, but I was in desperate need of comfort myself. On some level, I think we both suspected what was coming.

This time, someone met us at the airport. It was Uncle Ben, husband of Aunt Helen. This was also far out of context. We hadn't seen Uncle Ben for years. Dispatched by Dad on his unhappy errand, Uncle Ben greeted us with as much of a smile as he could muster. "Your dad thought you'd want to come right over to the hospital." He was the sweetest, kindest guy on the planet, but even Uncle Ben had difficulty being cheerful for us that day.

Mom was in the same room, but the world had shifted in the few days since Josh and I had kissed her goodbye and blithely left for New York. Unable to talk, smile at us, or even open her eyes, she was in a drug-induced stupor, hooked to machines. No one bothered to keep up the charade that she was okay. We could see that she was very, very sick—although still no one told us what she had.

Everyone around us was very serious and very quiet. There were lots of hushed voices and intense conversations. Doctors and nurses went in and out of her room constantly and we were allowed in only for short periods of time. We could only stand by the foot of Mom's bed, helplessly watching nothing happening.

I'm sure in our hearts we were hoping she would just wake up and smile at us, but deep down I could not ignore my inner unshakeable recognition of doom. I remember an overwhelming disconnection to the body I saw in that bed, so far removed from my reality of my mother that I didn't feel capable of crying, or even feeling.

Mostly we waited out in the hallway. People gave us pitying looks. Those poor children, I could hear them thinking.

On one of those days that I spent out in the hallway, a group of medical students accompanied a doctor into my mother's room. I couldn't help noticing that one of them was really cute.

Well-programmed to recognize potential boyfriend material, somehow I managed to engineer a conversation. I could tell he was interested, too. My mind leapt ahead. "I wonder if Mom would like him." Then I immediately shifted into guilt: Could I possibly be a more thoughtless daughter, thinking about boys at such a time? Could there possibly be a more grotesque start to a love story than meeting my future husband at my mother's deathbed? (That shameful start was avoided since I didn't end up dating this future doctor, but he did call and came to our house when we were sitting shiva.)

My sister, my brother, and I existed for a week in a real life Twilight Zone. After spending the days at gritty Jackson Memorial, at night we went back across the causeway to Miami Beach. Carla and I had shared a room our entire lives, but I can't remember what we talked about that week, or whether we talked much at all. No adults made any effort to distract, comfort, or counsel us. Three teenagers, separated by a total of five years and a few walls, we spent that week together in lonely, frightened isolation and confusion.

One night, as usual, the three of us were all tense when we got home from the hospital. Something happened that made me explode at Josh. Just 13, with a gravely ill mother, he was already scared, and scarred. Now suddenly, he became a target for his older, supposedly mature sister, who should have represented safety and security. My emotions spilled out like projectile vomit, unleashing fear, anger, and everything I had been accumulating all week.

My eruption didn't last long. But it added a few new emotions to my pile: guilt and shame. Streaming tears, I wrapped my arms around my brother, trying with a pathetic hug to erase the cruel words I had just hurled in his forlorn face. Josh accepted my apology and probably felt too scared and alone to give me what I deserved right back. He needed me. He never mentioned that incident and now says he has no memory of it.

But I do. That moment wedged into my psyche and my relationship with my brother, and it's still there. That outburst was the foundation for the shift from sister to surrogate mother. I had just taken my first psychology class freshman year, all I needed to form a lasting view of my brother's loss. My heart ached for his pain. I was eighteen, technically an adult, which made his need for Mom seem so much greater; he was losing five precious years I had already had. How could he ever recover? Today my brother is a successful doctor, but to me he is still that wounded, motherless boy who needed my protection and love to replace the mother he lost.

Back in 1968, those issues lay ahead as we shuttled between home and hospital, enclosed in a limbo zone until the bomb blast broke through the final fragile barrier.

The morning of July 4, we heard Dad's car pull into the carport around 8 a.m. The four of us came face to face in the hallway outside Josh's bedroom. Through tears, he hugged us close, and told us Mom had died that morning. Our strong invincible father was suddenly not the rock we had always known. I had never seen him so vulnerable; I had never believed he *was* vulnerable. He didn't give us details, but we didn't need any. It didn't matter. Nothing mattered. The worst had happened. Our lives would never be the same.

I never got to say goodbye.

Life Is Not Fair

Moms don't die. This couldn't be happening. Maybe it didn't feel real to my father, either. They didn't even own a cemetery plot.

The morning my mother died, Dad and I drove into Miami to choose a location in the Jewish cemetery. After looking at a few choices, Dad bought a section of plots together under a tree. We comforted ourselves with the idea that Mom, who religiously avoided the sun, would be in the shade. I would only get the irony years later when I found out she had died of melanoma.

Because my father was an observant Jew, according to the rules of burial, Mom's funeral needed to be held within 24 hours. My biggest problem was my garment bag, sitting in Monticello, New York, with all my dresses. Carla was two sizes smaller, so at the top of my list the day my mother died was borrowing a dress to wear to her funeral.

It never occurred to me to look through my mother's closet, although she was my size. Somehow it did not seem possible on that day to walk into her closet and touch her things.

Some people get rid of their loved ones' clothing so fast the Salvation Army truck shows up practically before the body is buried. Others leave the possessions untouched for years, as we did, just as Mom left them. I wasn't sure this was a good idea, but I would never have suggested to Dad that he think about clearing them out.

"Why don't you go through Mom's clothes and take what you want?" my father would ask me occasionally when I came home.

"I don't want anything." I was firm, I was sure, I was bitter. I took nothing.

Today, I would kill for those clothes. And not only because they would be vintage. They would be something tangible, something to touch, wear, smell. Sometimes I can remember the clothes Mom wore better than I can remember her face. Her shirtwaist dresses. The bright pink satin dress she wore one New Year's Eve. The white slim pants that reminded me of Jackie Kennedy.

Word spread among my friends, and anyone who was home that summer showed up at my mother's funeral or at our house while we sat shiva. Sitting shiva, the Jewish version of mourning, traditionally lasts a week. My father tore the lapel of his suit jacket and didn't shave. We were not allowed to wear anything leather. But the real tradition, as in every Jewish event, is the food.

Platters were ordered to feed the people who came to visit. And all those people brought more food. Cold cuts, casseroles, coffee cake, cookies, there is no limit to what people bring because Jews drown our sorrows in food, not drink. I was definitely drowning that week. I remember it vividly because—and this was historic—my father did NOT comment on or even notice how much I ate.

Our house, missing the person who made it a home, was filled with friends and family. Talking with them, I was polite and courteous; but what came out of my mouth was far from what really was going on in my head.

Of all the people here, all the people I know, why was it **my** *mother who had to die? And if one of my parents had to die, why couldn't it be Dad instead of Mom?*

I would never have said these thoughts out loud to anyone. Even thinking this meant I was a terrible person. But I didn't care; I thought it anyway. My mother was tender; my father was terrifying, and not just to me. He terrified his employees. My friends. My dates. Now he was all I had.

I didn't know a single person whose mother had died. It went against every law of the universe. It was unthinkable that this could happen to my beautiful, vibrant mother.

I never signed up for this...

I'd had an entitled and easy life. This didn't fit with how it was supposed to be.

Life. Is. Not. Fair. This was the first time that I faced that truth.

But I didn't stop to think about it. We weren't into thinking back then, weren't into introspection, or how to process grief or loss. No one suggested a therapist, or how to adjust to being suddenly motherless. I just coped. We all coped.

The day after we finished sitting shiva, my father sent my brother and me back to camp. My bunk of 14 year old girls, my garment bag, and Mel were all waiting for me. With the incredible resilience of youth, I stepped back into life.

Life meant accepting and adapting to the new normal, a vast black hole blasted into the center of our family. Mostly I didn't experience the gaping Grand Canyon up close. I came home only on brief trips, my life no longer centered in Miami Beach. During her one remaining year at home, Carla had a serious boyfriend and was looking ahead to college, so her life was busy and distracted. It was Josh who came home every day from school to a house without light. Josh who had to live without hugs and kisses. Josh who had a father who loved him but who didn't know how to be a mother.

As a surrogate mother, I took on the role but never could fill the hole. I was completely unprepared and mostly uninterested in this aspect of my family responsibility, and not very capable of guiding anyone else through the treacherous waters of adolescence. Mostly I was there in a crisis, when circumstances called for my involvement—to talk to Josh, or try to be a comforting female presence in his life.

Losing Mom cut my father off at the knees. Surrounded by broken pieces, he picked himself up and plunged into life as the father of three teenagers, giving me a remarkable role model for resilience.

Early on I had little appreciation, but as I got older, I developed a deep admiration for how Dad took on this new unwanted job for which he was so unprepared. He was aware of his plight, aware that he didn't measure up, aware that with all his intelligence he was missing the inherent softness and instinctual wisdom that had made his wife so beloved and brilliant a mother. He knew all this and he tried to fix it.

He took on parenting with the characteristic determination that marked the rest of his life. My father was the go-to guy, he was where the buck stopped. People looked to him for jobs, for leadership, for money, for advice, all of which he gave on a regular basis.

Being a parent meant giving even more. Dad seemed capable of unlimited giving and never taking. He never felt sorry for himself; he never complained. He was always trying to do more, help more, to apply the force of his iron will to being the only parent we had. He asked nothing of us in return. He was at every event or occasion in our lives, happy or sad, trying to mask what he was really feeling—*their mother should be here*. For whatever mistakes he made when we were younger, no one could possibly fault the efforts he made once Mom died.

Dad was 12 years older than Mom, 53 when she died. Once I asked him why he didn't marry again. I wanted him to be happy. By then I could see that my father would have been a great catch.

He shook his head. "That's always complicated. You kids come first and I want you to feel secure about that. If I married someone else, a new wife might come between me and my children. I could never allow that." He had a female companion for more than twenty years, but he kept their life mostly separate from his life with us. Although he outlived my mother by 35 years, he never married again.

16 *Words*

According to Jewish tradition, there's about a year between the time of death and the formal unveiling ceremony of the stone in the cemetery. A few months after Mom died, Dad asked me what I thought we should engrave on the stone that would mark her grave.

The day she was buried was the only time I'd ever set foot in a cemetery. But I knew what most of the stones said: Rest in Peace...Forever in Our Hearts...Beloved Wife, Mother, Daughter, Sister. All those things were true, but none of those words seemed to capture the essence of my mom.

As the oldest of her three children, I took it as a serious responsibility to help decide how she should be remembered for eternity. I was in college, and I spent far more time on this assignment than on any of my term papers until I came across something I thought was perfect: words that had been written 300 years earlier by John Milton.

It was an out-of-the-box idea, and I was surprised that my very traditional dad agreed.

Over the years I've sometimes looked back at words I wrote, feeling they could be changed or edited or improved. But not these words. This decision was set in stone. Just 16 words—and I still think they are perfect:

"Grace was in all her steps, Heaven in her eyes, In every gesture dignity and love."
John Milton's words are the essence of my mother.

Losing a beloved mother is hard at any age. Having it happen so early and so suddenly was traumatic, terrifying, an enormous broken piece. I wasn't even capable of appreciating or assessing the magnitude of my loss. The aftermath of death simply meant damage control. For the first time I was required to recalibrate, rebound, readjust and rearrange the composition of my life. The instincts for resilience were in me, I just hadn't needed to exercise them much. With Mom gone, I had to call upon my ability to adapt.

Despite a heavy dose of reality, I still clung to the hope that life would deliver the fantasies found in fairy tales. At the very least, I thought I deserved better treatment from the universe. Sometimes the universe comes through. The dark time around my mother's death was followed by a phase that was as close as I would get to a fairy tale.

Women in a Male Society

A few months after Mom died, I was back at Cornell for sophomore year when I heard that after almost 300 years of all-male history, and against the outrage of many alumni and students, Yale College decided to admit women for the upcoming year. For future freshman and a few sophomore and junior transfers, it was a chance to be a real life Cinderella in an educational fairy tale.

The best and brightest girls on American campuses threw their names into arguably the most prestigious college admissions sweepstakes ever. Those who emerged from that rigorous selection process would walk away with the first undergraduate Yale diplomas awarded to women.

Like thousands of coeds all over the country, I sent in an application to transfer. I wasn't optimistic—with C's in Geology freshman year, I was a real longshot. The odds seemed even slimmer and my hopes even dimmer that spring, when I read the cover story of the *New York Times Magazine*, describing the ridiculously competitive Yale admissions process and the over-achieving "superwomen" who would soon get letters anointing them the chosen few.

A few days later I stood in my dorm room holding one of those acceptance letters, feeling like I just won the lottery. Ecstatic as I was, I was equally sure there had been a huge mistake.

Feeling far from a superwoman, I arrived at Yale four months later, in September 1969. News media swarmed the campus. My hometown paper, *The Miami Herald*, flew a reporter and photographer up to New Haven to interview me and two other women from south Florida. I began to appreciate that Yale coeducation was a significant milestone, and I was part of it.

Today it seems hard to imagine and almost quaint to remember what Yale was like when we arrived. The guide for incoming students recommended that we "treat Yale as you would treat a woman." Men swam naked in the gym pool. Busloads of girls arrived every weekend from Smith, Wellesley and Vassar for mixers with Yale men.

When a few hundred women moved into the ivy-covered colleges and merged into the population of 4,000 men, the impact was immediate. A completely coeducational campus would take years, but some minor shake-ups occurred overnight. Full length mirrors were installed in dorm bathrooms. The new "superwomen" were stared at and scrutinized. In classes, I felt pressure to say something super-smart every time I opened my mouth.

Typical of the time, I went to college with an unspoken understanding that after graduation, I would come home with a husband. I couldn't have been better positioned in the potential husband pool. At Cornell, the ratio of men to women was 4 to 1. Overwhelmingly male Yale was beyond the jackpot, and I'm not proud to admit that I prioritized what Yale offered socially above what it offered academically. My father's pressure to get higher grades in high school did not indicate he held higher aspirations for me. Dad used to tell people that I was majoring in boys; and he wasn't all wrong.

Once I got to Yale I was always surrounded by boys. My friends and I went to Washington to march against the Vietnam War in October 1969.

Social life aside, in a sense, we women were very motivated lab rats in a prestigious educational experiment. Coeducation was a magnificent gesture in the midst of a turbulent time. In my two years at Yale, my classmates and I were caught up in the biggest upheaval of our generation, when political activism, sexual freedom, feminism, and enormous social change all collided. Yale was a microcosm of what was starting to happen in American society.

Decades later, I discovered that I wasn't the only woman who had arrived at Yale wondering: *How did I get in?* Some insight into the answer came from the perfect source. Just like

Cinderella, our fairy tale featured a fairy godmother. Elga Wasserman, J.D. and Ph.D., was Dean of Coeducation. Her wisdom and leadership spearheaded the transition. At the time of coeducation she wrote, "Women students need an unusual sense of self to persevere in a predominantly male setting."

Years later, Mrs. Wasserman was a special guest at a luncheon I attended, commemorating 40 years since Yale had admitted women. She was asked how the Admissions staff had chosen a few hundred girls from many thousands who applied. What were the qualities determined to be most important for success at Yale?

The challenge for the committee, she said, was having to choose women who would arrive on campus without knowing what they would find. So Yale sought women best equipped to handle whatever they would have to face. Her answer finally gave me a clue about how I got in with those C's in Geology.

"No shrinking violets," Mrs. Wasserman said. Grades, scores, and accomplishments were not always at the top of the list. What they were looking for, she explained, were women who had an indefinable quality of independence or pioneer spirit, who would be able to cope and handle themselves in the heavily male environment without being overwhelmed and overridden. She was describing *resilience and adaptability*: characteristics which allow us to evolve, to adapt to change, circumstance, crisis and whatever else life throws at us.

At 20, it's doubtful I would have appreciated the wisdom of that strategy, but I do now. Adaptability is the quality that has served me best, not only at Yale, but with all the other things in life I never signed up for.

I did sign up for a memorable course, when the title leapt out at me from the catalogue senior year: *Women in a Male Society* seemed to perfectly describe me and my female classmates. A seminar with 20 students, it was taught by a psychologist at the Yale Child Study Center, the only woman professor I had at Yale.

Women's Studies didn't exist yet, not at Yale nor anywhere else. Even as an American history major who wrote my junior and senior essays on women's issues, I wasn't well-informed. The modern feminist movement was still in its infancy, *Ms. Magazine* still a year away from its first issue with the famous description of the "click" moment.

My own click moment was an encounter with a *New York Times* reporter who stopped me on my way to registration on the first day of school and asked, "Do you think women *deserve* to be at Yale?" Clearly, he didn't.

If that incident was a click, the seminar was a sonic boom. The reading and discussions provided an immersive introduction to feminism—the thinking, the politics, the people that were changing the world for me, my

Nothing made my dad prouder than having a "Yale man" in the family. Taken at graduation June 1971.

classmates, for all women. For me it was a beginning and an end. The seminar helped me gel thoughts and feelings germinating from the moment I set foot on campus. What an ideal way to end my Yale experience, taking what I learned out into the real world where all of us would be *Women in a Male Society*.

After graduation, I would learn that a Yale degree didn't magically open doors; women still had to pound on them. My experience at Yale gave me the confidence to believe that I *could*. And that I *should*.

I graduated with honors but without a husband on the horizon. The vast majority of my female classmates went on to law school, medical school, or grad school. I might have pursued women's studies if it had existed, but without a passion for any intellectual pursuit, I had no plan in place. Instead, I spent a year working at two place-holder jobs in Boston. Still unsure about a career or even my next move, the summer of 1972 provided the perfect scenario, especially for a political junkie.

The Vietnam War had put the presidency up for grabs and unleashed an idealistic generation learning to use political power. At their convention in Miami Beach, the Democrats nominated George McGovern for president a few blocks away from where I grew up. After scoring a ticket, I wedged into the crowd on the convention floor, where I ended the evening standing just a few feet away from the new nominee at the podium as he delivered his acceptance speech. Whether it was the politics, the power, or the proximity, I was inspired, intoxicated, infused with purpose.

I had found something worthy I wanted to sign up for. Filled with passion to change the world, I went to McGovern campaign headquarters in Washington, D.C., where I met with campaign officials, presenting myself as a Yale graduate and an American history major, willing to go anywhere in the entire United States as a McGovern volunteer. I didn't care about a title, a salary, or anything else. All I wanted was to contribute to the downfall of Richard Nixon.

No thanks, they told me.

The McGovern campaign wasn't known for brilliant strategy, still I was shocked that they would turn me down. Fortunately, my resilience kicked in. This rejection turned into a life-altering fork in my road, directed by dumb luck and the spirit of adaptability recognized by the Yale admissions committee. There I was, in the downtown Washington office building that housed the entire McGovern campaign. There had to be somewhere in that 10-story building I could be useful. I started down from the top, wandering from floor to floor, peeking into offices and asking for a chance to work. Advance. Speechwriting. Scheduling. I got nowhere.

A receptionist was sitting right in the hallway when I stepped out of the elevator on the third floor. "Press" was printed on the sign over her head. "What does a press person do?" I asked her. Yale graduate or not, I had no idea.

I gave her the same little pitch I'd been trying on the floors above. "Does anyone need help? I'll work for free."

The receptionist made a call, I was ushered into an office, and within a few minutes I met a young woman my age, who became my new boss and is still a treasured friend. I spent an intense and intoxicating few months as Assistant State Press Coordinator, working as a campaign volunteer days and nights and weekends. Besides my father, what subsidized my idealism was a well-paid week of work as an extra on *The Exorcist,* shooting in Georgetown during that time.

And what a time to be in the nation's capital, during the early emerging Watergate stories written by Woodward and Bernstein in the *Washington Post.* Living inside the bubble of idealism that immersed and isolated us working on the campaign, all that mattered was that we were changing the world. At least I thought so until the election, when I had to recover from the shock of losing every single state except my current home state of Massachusetts.

Meanwhile I learned what press people did and how important they were. Everything we did in the campaign seemed to be focused on getting press coverage, particularly on television. Instead of trying to get someone's attention, I could switch sides. I decided that for me, that was a better place to be.

I had no experience or insight into what it meant to be part of the press, other than working on my high school yearbook. Just before senior year, I had spent a summer studying journalism at Northwestern with other high school students, yet I had not pursued writing in college. But now, I thought I saw where things were pointing, and that's where I pointed myself.

This idea also fit my style as a fly-by-the-seat-of-my-pants type, not a planner. My new *plan* was to return to Boston with a vague strategy that involved trying to "get into television."

Since I owed my dad a visit, first I flew to Miami to spend some time with him. While I was there, I figured maybe I could (or should) learn a little bit about my future vocation. After all, I had never set foot inside a TV station. My uncle knew someone at the Miami CBS affiliate and he arranged a meeting for me in the News Department. I met with the Assistant to the WTVJ News Director and offered to work a few weeks for free.

She turned me down.

Déjà vu? This was a repeat of my experience at McGovern headquarters six months earlier. Whatever I had to offer, I couldn't even *give* it away.

She did throw me a crumb, suggesting I go over to the Public Affairs Department. Maybe they could use me.

The news department, part of the Wometco complex, was housed in its own small one-story building. This time there was no 10-story building I could roam around, hoping to find someone more receptive. I was very politely ushered out the door and onto the street.

Dismissed and disappointed, I emerged into the bright sunshine of downtown Miami. Walking along the sidewalk towards the corner, I realized Public Affairs was in a building located across the street from where I had parked. I knew my meter was about to run out, and any minute I would get a ticket.

Nearing the crosswalk, I hesitated, thinking this entire excursion was a total waste of time. What was Public Affairs, anyway? I had no idea.

So I made a random decision: If I got to the corner and the light stayed green, I would cross the street, go to my car, avoid the ticket, and forget about "getting into television" till I got back to Boston. If the light turned red, I'd enter the building and stop by the Public Affairs Department.

I had no idea that once again I was at a significant crossroads of my life. Could the symbolism possibly be more obvious? This time, I was literally *standing at a crossroads.*

The light turned red. I stepped into the Public Affairs Department and a whole new world.

I entered the building, and the television industry, at the ideal moment. Television news was in its golden age. The three networks ruled the airwaves, and the evening broadcasts were the jewels in their crowns. Walter Cronkite was still in his seat; Dan Rather and Tom Brokaw were covering the White House. CNN was not even a figment of Ted Turner's imagination. Celebrity journalism was far off in the future. ET did not exist, not as a syndicated show or as an alien.

I not only showed up at the right time, but also at the right place. Miami was a growing, diverse metropolitan area and a great news town. CBS was the premier network, and WTVJ had dominated the local scene since the invention of television.

I knew none of this when I walked in the door. I did not own a TV set, and never watched TV in college. Just as I had entered the McGovern press office having no idea what a press person did, I entered the Public Affairs Department with no idea what it was.

It turned out Public Affairs was intended to serve the community. Chiefly it did this by producing *Montage*, a 30 minute local version of *60 Minutes.* Run by Public Affairs Director/Executive Producer Joe Abrell, and unlike most public affairs shows, *Montage* had a great time slot and top ratings. The host was Ralph Renick, a TV institution who had anchored the news broadcasts since WTVJ first went on the air the year I was born.

Like the national news media, the *Montage* staff and WTVJ were primarily white and male, another factor that made it the ideal moment for me to join the television industry. Yale had prepared me well for being a woman in a male society. Being surrounded by men wasn't at all intimidating, it was my comfort zone.

Once again I was stepping into a situation that required adaptation, kind of like being thrown into the deep end of the pool head first when you don't know how to swim. If I didn't want to drown, I'd have to learn television production on the fly, which I did. Almost immediately Joe had me writing scripts. My agreement to work a few weeks for free not only got me in the door but allowed me to stay in the room.

Within a few weeks it turned out that having a Yale degree was not as useful as having a uterus. The Supreme Court handed down a landmark decision, *Roe vs. Wade*, and Public Affairs committed to produce a half hour show devoted to abortion. With such highly controversial and sensitive material, it wouldn't do for one of the male producers to walk into abortion clinics and interview young pregnant women. This situation called for some estrogen.

Within less than a year, I was producing, writing, and reporting my own segments, though being on the air myself was not a goal and didn't occur to me until Joe suggested it. Even further afield was the concept of living in Miami permanently. *I never signed up for this...* and I never did move back to Boston.

Joe guided his staff with a light touch, though he did point out that I conducted my first on-camera interview in the field while visibly holding against my chest the large black film magazine for the camera. And now that I was going to be a professional woman on the air, he suggested maybe it was time to get rid of the waist-length hair and hippie college wardrobe. Point taken.

My work time was split between shooting stories out in the field and writing and editing back at the station. Despite some initial grumbling from one guy about having a woman on the staff, the atmosphere in the *Montage* office was casual, congenial, and cooperative. I was too green to appreciate how rare this was as a working environment.

I wasn't just learning about television, I was *learning*. Every story meant becoming a mini-expert on a new subject, and meeting interesting new people. Celebrities were often *Montage* studio guests, interviewed on our set by Joe; and I met people from Rose Kennedy to Sammy Davis, Jr. to Mother Teresa. One day Joe was going out of town, so he assigned the studio interview to me. This was way out of my comfort zone, and I was nervous. No worries, he told me, it was just some young director neither of us had ever heard of, who had a new movie coming out. The movie was *Jaws*; the director was Steven Spielberg.

Joe used to predict we would look back someday and consider this the best job we would ever have. Like many *Montage* alumni, I have to admit that he was absolutely right. Joe encouraged us to explore, grow, and freed us to do our best creative work. He allowed me to dive into sensitive, controversial subjects like rape and breast cancer, which at the time were considered taboo for television.

Betty Ford had not yet been diagnosed with breast cancer and few people knew much about it, when the local chapter of the American Cancer Society approached *Montage* to shed some light by doing a segment on the subject. As the only woman on the staff, it's no surprise the assignment ended up on my desk. The surprises came later, once I grasped the significance of the story and asked Joe to let me devote more time to it.

Back then, simply getting women with breast cancer to show their faces publicly on television was considered a minor accomplishment. With the help of some courageous women, our story pushed the envelope further.

What started out as a short segment for *Montage* turned into a groundbreaking documentary about breast cancer that I produced and wrote. Just two years after the day I first walked into his office, Joe sent me to Philadelphia to accept a national Clarion Award from Women in Communications for community service.

The World Turns

Until the *Montage* segment, I had little knowledge or interest in cancer professionally or personally. It was five years after my mother's death when I finally would learn that cancer had a very personal connection to me.

The word *cancer* was never spoken in my presence during the months my mother was in the hospital. It was never mentioned at her funeral, or by any of the friends or family who came to our house while we were sitting shiva. It was never mentioned by my father, sister, or brother, even in the privacy of our home, even in the years afterward.

By the time I was working in Miami television, my sister and brother were both gone, leaving my dad alone in an empty nest. I'm sure having me nearby must have been comforting.

Raised Orthodox, Dad also found comfort in the Jewish traditions. Looking back, it makes sense that he chose Yom Kippur, the Day of Atonement, to shed something that must have burdened his soul.

We attended Temple Emanuel's morning services, held as always on High Holy days in the Miami Beach Auditorium. During a break, Dad and I walked over to his office at the Nautilus Hotel. He sat behind his desk, I settled into one of the chairs facing him. I expected we'd just sit and relax, but Dad had an agenda, and he got right to the point.

"I want to tell you something about Mom."

I was stunned even before hearing what "something" was. Dad wasn't chatty, or very communicative about personal things. Clearly this talk had a serious purpose.

"You remember Mom used to be careful about being in the sun?"

I nodded, though I had never considered the obvious contradiction until this instant. Though countless family photos documented her lifelong love for the water and the beach, at some point Mom had started wearing hats and using parasols, saying she was "allergic" to the sun. She hadn't urged us to cover up or avoid the sun, and I never questioned her about it.

Dad was calm and reflective as he told me the story that finally revealed the truth.

In her thirties, Mom had discovered a suspicious-looking mole on her back. Being careful and cautious, she'd consulted a dermatologist, who recommended a biopsy. When the biopsy results came back, the surgeon told my mother not to worry, she was fine, end of story.

Only it wasn't the end; more accurately it was the beginning of the end. Mom didn't worry until she had reason to worry, several years later when she was diagnosed with cancer. Investigating to determine the primary source, her doctors found early indications of melanoma on the slide of the biopsy from the mole. Had it been read properly, or had she gotten a second opinion, my mother would have had another simple surgery and lived to raise her children. Instead, by the time cancer was diagnosed, it had spread throughout her body.

Five years after her death, the emotions still had not faded for my father, who cried as he recalled his desperation and helplessness. "I took her everywhere, to every specialist. They tried everything, but no one could save her."

All this had been going on while I was sent off to Cornell and enjoyed my freshman year, oblivious.

"Why didn't you tell me?" I asked Dad.

"She didn't want you to know."

"But why not?"

"What good would it have done? You were young; she wanted the three of you to be able to live your lives."

My mind flashed on little things—being sent to move into my college dorm alone, my parents never visiting Ithaca, Mom in her bed jacket waiting for me to come home from the airport freshman year.

"She was so proud that you were at Cornell. She would be so proud to watch you on television," my father told me.

In my mid-twenties, I was still too young to fully appreciate the loss—hers, his, and ours. Dimly, very dimly, right there in my father's office, all the pain started to dawn on me.

His pain. He had carried this alone all these years.

"I never imagined she would die before me. And I couldn't save her." He sounded bereft.

Her pain. "How did she hide it? How could she stand seeing us and not saying anything?"

Our pain. All for nothing.

A *mistake*. I had never considered the concept that doctors were capable of such human error.

"Why didn't you sue somebody?"

"What would that have accomplished? It couldn't bring her back."

Dad stood up from behind his desk and came around to my side where I sat, trying to absorb the news that rocked my world. He was tender as he gazed at me and stroked my hair, murmuring, "Marcella's daughter."

That's what he often said to us kids at times of his greatest emotion, as if to remind himself that he still had a piece of her, that the three of us were the way in which she lived on for him.

We walked from his office the few blocks back to Yom Kippur services. I had stopped trusting in a God who could have allowed my mother to die. Learning what had actually happened made even less sense. I sat with my father as we chanted the prayers I had heard all my life, having even less faith in their meaning, their importance or their value.

After services, I went back to my apartment. When I looked in the mirror, suddenly my great tan didn't seem like such a great idea. I was a prime candidate for melanoma. All those weekends I spent sitting outside by the apartment pool were crossed off my list.

I loaded up on sunscreen. That took care of the outside. On the inside, it was a different story.

Mr. Hollywood

I hadn't even reached puberty when I first asked Mom, "How will I know when I meet the right man?" With a serene smile, she repeated the magic words mothers have sold their daughters through the ages: "You'll just **know**."

My sister asked my mother the same question and got the same answer. At 15, Carla did **know:** that her first boyfriend Paul was the love of her life. Just 18 months older, I was maybe 18 boyfriends ahead of Carla when she married Paul at age 21. With a front row seat for 40 years at their amazingly happy marriage, it's always astounded me. How was she *smart* enough to choose the right husband at 15? Especially when I got better grades?

It took me nearly twice as long as my sister to settle on a guy.

That time frame didn't escape the notice of the most important guy in my life. After a few years of me appearing on the air, Dad loved to brag that he was now known in the local community as "Darryle Pollack's father." But his pride didn't change his priorities. He told me in no uncertain terms that at this point in my life, I should be more focused on having a family. In my late 20's, I was, according to Dad, overly career-oriented.

He wasn't all wrong. I was working 7 days a week, for Public Affairs weekdays and for the news department on weekends to expand my experience. I had boyfriends but not a marriage mindset. Plus all that reading in feminism and women's studies had taken root in my soul. I had seen no shining examples of women who had managed successful careers simultaneously with successful families. My sister was already pregnant, while I had begun to believe I might never want children at all.

It wasn't for personal reasons but for career opportunity that I made the permanent switch to a normal work week, leaving Public Affairs for News, working for the same people who had rejected me as a free intern a few years earlier. The move to news fulltime meant more recognition, and stepping into the center of the action.

Murders, movie stars, meeting Presidents of the United States was all part of the job. Occasional big stories could land us on the CBS network news. Famous names and faces on the presidential campaign trail were regular visitors to the newsroom during an election year, and I got to pal around with people who were my heroes, like Hunter S. Thompson and R.W. Apple of the *New York Times*.

Interviewing Watergate burglar and artist Howard Hunt,
with my cameraman, Larry Greene, in 1977.

As a woman on the air, part of the deal meant accepting the importance of appearance—my clothes, my makeup, my jewelry, my body, and most of all, my hair—got an excessive amount of attention. Everything was fair game for my bosses and viewers. None of that ever felt natural—and I never got used to it.

Yet even with mixed feelings about being a public figure, I had stumbled into the perfect career for my talents and my personality. Constantly changing stories, learning a little about a lot, suited my nature. Being on the late news was the perfect schedule for my body clock. My station dominated the ratings in the Miami market; and I appeared on the top-rated shows. My superiors were eager to promote and showcase my work, giving me freedom to develop series and stories that interested me, and to make an impact. I couldn't wait to get to work every day.

I never signed up for this… like going to Yale, my television career put a supremely positive spin on those words. I had fallen into a fairy tale that continued to unfold.

At the peak of his career, Henry Winkler as the Fonz was the hottest character on television. His first movie, *Heroes*, was about to open in Miami and I was assigned to cover the premiere for the late news. My nightly live roundup in the studio called *Who's in the News* was my personal contribution to the coming explosion in celebrity journalism—not that it's something to brag about.

At Dadeland Mall hundreds of kids pushed and screamed, trying to get a little piece of the Fonz. My crew and I were surrounded and carried along until we were shoved practically on top of Mr. Cool himself. I stuck my microphone in his face. So did the other reporters, but I was the only female and he directed his attention to me.

"How do you like this screaming and shoving?" It was a stupid question, but Winkler was smiling and polite.

"It's my life. It's pretty exciting, isn't it?"

"What do you do when you want to escape?"

He paused a beat, gave me a huge smile and a snappy line. "I ask you out to dinner."

My snappy comeback was to nudge closer with a flirty smile and hook my arm through Winkler's. "Okay, let's go!"

As soon as my cameraman had the shot, the mob moved in and my theoretical dinner date was carried away by the surging kids. Still, the brief encounter was fun and had its value. Back at work, my station played up the story on the late news. The next morning, the *Miami Herald* ran a piece about Winkler asking me for a date.

I figured that would be my one brush with Hollywood.

Not quite.

That same morning the office called, asking me to come in early. That's how I learned the Fonz was not the only celebrity in town. In fact, Winkler was the dimmest (in celebrity wattage) of the stars who would be accepting awards from NATO, the National Organization of Theater Owners. They were meeting on Miami Beach, giving out awards for Stars of the Year. As the station's designated celebrity expert, I would cover the story.

Apparently other reporters were angling for this assignment. It wasn't that they were big fans of the Fonz, or Sylvester Stallone, the biggest new star of the year, or Mel Brooks, who would also be there. These were male reporters, who wanted a chance for a close-up with the one female star being honored: Sophia Loren.

My nighttime crew was called in early, and the station arranged for a private interview with Mel Brooks. This was a big bonus for my cameraman, Larry Greene. A colorful character and even in his early twenties practically a legend himself, "Leapin' Larry" was a big Mel Brooks fan. He brought along a box of Raisinets, knowing Mel was famously addicted.

At the press conference at the Fontainebleau Hotel, I didn't cross paths again with the Fonz, but I did verify that Sophia Loren is as breathtaking in person as on film. Interviewing Mel was a kick, mostly because Larry was thrilled to meet him and hand over the Raisinets.

The guy with Mel handed over his card and asked me to send a videotape of the interview to him in Los Angeles. At the cocktail reception soon afterwards, the same guy sought me out again and struck up another conversation.

As a young woman working in TV news, I was used to this. I assumed he was Mel's PR guy; either he wanted to represent me or he was hitting on me. Pretty soon I had my answer, and somehow I found myself agreeing to meet him later that night back at the Fontainebleau for a drink, after the late news.

"I couldn't think of an excuse fast enough," I told John Neuharth, my producer, when I got back to the station. "I'm not gonna show up."

"You should go," John urged. "Maybe Mel will be there, too."

Nah, I told him. I met plenty of celebrities on the job, the Fontainebleau was a half hour away, and the Hollywood guy wasn't my type.

But he called me to confirm just as I was rushing up to the studio for the 11 p.m. news broadcast. Who calls to confirm an hour before a date? Caught off guard, I couldn't quite say "Oops, I was planning to stand you up!" So after the broadcast, I headed back to the Fontainebleau.

Mr. Hollywood was waiting in the circular driveway outside the hotel. Climbing into my car, he told me we were going to a popular nightspot, The Cricket Club. A private club, it was very trendy, very loud, not my style, and not nearby. But there was a plus to his plan. Earlier, Mel had asked what he was doing later on. And since Mel remembered me from the interview, he invited himself along on our date.

Score for my producer.

Soon after we arrived at the club Mel joined us, and the club had us all pose for pictures, ecstatic with the coup.

Mel's personality was way too big to confine to our booth. For several hours, he worked the whole room. When you're on a date with Mel Brooks, the laughs and the patter and the jokes never stop. I found out that Mr. Hollywood's name was Howard,

I could see that he had a great sense of humor, but we barely had a chance to say two words to each other.

At 3 a.m. we finally got up to leave; and found out that Mel had dismissed his car and driver, assuming we'd take him back to the Fontainebleau with us. So the three of us headed back to Miami Beach in my car—me driving, Howard next to me, and Mel in the back seat.

Even with jet lag, Mel was wired in the middle of the night, and the chatter continued nonstop. Until suddenly Mel changed his tone and a new side of him emerged. Leaning forward between the two bucket seats, he aimed a pointed question right at me.

"So. You got a boyfriend?"

It was the Jewish inquisition.

I hesitated and mumbled the truth. "Um…Kind of."

Now in Jewish father mode, Mel pounced. "You don't sound very excited. Why don't you dump this boyfriend, marry Howard, and move to California?"

This got me so flustered that I missed the turnoff for the exit to Miami Beach and had to get off the highway to turn around. The guys had no idea where we were, but I did—in the most dangerous neighborhood of Miami—nowhere you'd want to be at 3 a.m. I could already picture the newspaper headline: *Miami Reporter Causes Injury to Beloved Comic Mel Brooks in Freeway Mishap.*

I managed to get us safely back to the Fontainebleau, where Mel said goodnight and left us. And at 4 a.m. I finally got a chance to talk to my date, sitting on a couch in the hotel lobby. Howard wasn't Mel's PR guy, but his personal manager, I found out. (I didn't find out what a personal manager actually was.) I also learned that he had never been married and was pretty funny, although Mel is a hard act to follow.

The night Mel Brooks made a match. October 28, 1977.

We sat in the lobby talking until 6 a.m. Saturday morning. "I wouldn't normally ask you this, but we live so far apart and I'd love to get to know you better. Mel and I are supposed to fly to New York today but I don't really have to be there until Monday," Howard continued. "You mentioned you've never been to Key West. How about if I change my plans and we drive down there for the weekend?"

Whoa! This was not in the script. I told him I'd think about it and call him back by 9 a.m. Then I left. He was convinced he would never see me again.

But I'd already decided to go. It wasn't love at first sight. It wasn't even really romantic. My thinking was more like something you'd see in *Cosmopolitan* magazine (in the pre-AIDS era) at the top of the list of 10 Things You Should Do Just Once In Your Life: Have an Adventure with a Mysterious Stranger.

This was my chance. I'd sneak off for the weekend, he'd go back to Hollywood, I'd never see him again, and no one would ever know about it.

I went home and packed a bag for Key West.

Three months later, I took Mel's advice: I married Howard, and moved to California.

Married February 10, 1978, in Davie, Florida.

Not Eating My Words

Talk about living the fairy tale.

Not just a modern version of fairy tales, this was almost a duplication of a real life romance closer to home. My dad had been twelve years older than my mom, Howard was ten years older than me. Swept off her feet, my mom married my dad just a few months after they met. I did the same thing. Our cross-country commuter courtship was such a whirlwind, Howard used to joke that until after the wedding, we'd never seen each other on a Wednesday.

The swiftness didn't faze me since I had always idealized my parents' marriage. But I never knew Mom's true feelings about her quick courtship and marriage, and I wondered what advice she might have had about mine.

The beginning of married life was a blissful blur. I was so busy I didn't even look for a job right away. Arriving in Los Angeles just in time for Awards season, I attended the Golden Globes and the Oscars, thanks to Howard's nominated clients Anne Bancroft and Larry Gelbart. I tagged along on frequent business trips; I saw Dom DeLuise perform his nightclub act so many times, I knew it by heart.

After finding a job at the local CBS station, I started making a few friends at work and making my way around the huge city. Just a few miles from my door, I discovered something that made my adjustment to California infinitely smoother—and sweeter. It was a tiny little shop in the heart of Beverly Hills.

In those days before anyone thought of adding things like sea salt, bacon, and chili, Kron's Chocolatier was the epitome of elite chocolate. In addition to creative combinations (my favorite was fresh orange sections dipped in chocolate), they also made clever items out of chocolate—women's torsos, legs, records (before CDs or iPods), and telephones (before cellphones).

Best of all, they offered free samples. This was the obvious place to go for a gift for my new husband.

They sold what they called chocolate telegrams (another relic from the past)—personalized messages inscribed on a slab of chocolate, which came in a little wooden box. I ordered one, brought it home, and couldn't wait to give it to him. My agenda was crystal clear in the message inscribed in icing: "In honor of your wedding, you have my permission to eat this."

Kron's chocolate telegram, bought in Beverly Hills in 1978.

Around me, chocolate has a very short shelf life. Whatever the quantity, it rarely lasts longer than 24 hours. Anyone who knows me also knows about my clutter. I'm sentimental and I save everything. Chocolate is the only thing that I *don't* save.

Howard was the opposite—not a clutterer, not a saver. So go figure: I wanted to eat it, he wanted to save it—out of sentiment. He put the wooden box in the refrigerator.

It sat there, torturing me, calling me even with the refrigerator door closed. Yet even in my worst moments of chocolate desperation, I NEVER violated the sanctity of that chocolate.

The telegram remained untouched through the second winter of our marriage, when a weeklong deluge of rain sent the hillside behind our home sliding down, seeping underneath sliding doors and depositing 500 tons of mud onto the back patio. It sat at home when we traveled abroad to Spain, Italy, the Far East. The telegram was still there when we took a 6-week weekend course at UCLA designed to help couples make a decision about whether or not to have children. It remained unnoticed in the refrigerator when our decision resulted in the birth of our first child, Alison. And the chocolate telegram made the move with our family of three to our new home when our daughter was 2.

Even *before* Alli's birth, I qualified as a helicopter parent. Possibly I was the original helicopter parent, since the term hadn't been invented yet. In all honesty I deserved a stronger term, because *hovering* would have been a relatively benign descriptor of my mothering. Obsessive, neurotic, paranoid…a little closer.

Maybe no one was more surprised than I was by the emergence of a world-class worrywart from my formerly easygoing personality. Anxiety had been a gradual development, having legitimate roots in learning the circumstances of my mother's death. I think the most likely explanation is that by simply allowing myself to love someone, I risked losing them.

When I met Mel Brooks, he was promoting his movie *High Anxiety*. My own version rose to the surface around the same time, just after I married Howard and moved to California. I didn't discriminate among potential disasters from car accidents to earthquakes, but it was the specter of cancer that haunted me most, like an evil presence I could sense in the shadows stalking me.

On the outside I appeared normal, and my neurotic tendencies were noticed mostly by my husband and my doctors. Knowing that doctors made monumental mistakes made me a picky and prickly patient, with all body parts in play. A stomach pain could signal colon cancer, a headache was a potential brain tumor. Scientists hadn't yet proven genetic links to various cancers, but I suspected they would. Due to my mother's melanoma, most of my paranoia was focused on my skin.

On the receiving end was Dr. Arnold Klein, the celebrity dermatologist whose office assistant Debbie Rowe carried two of Michael Jackson's children. Every time he saw me, which was often, Dr. Klein would enter the examining room with a big smile and greet me with the same line: "So what do you have today that you think is cancer?" We'd both laugh, and he would put on his little headlamp that made him look like a coal miner and look at me under the bright lights.

I had been in California just two years the day I showed him a tiny spot on the side of my nose. This time he didn't laugh. He did a biopsy. The good news was that it wasn't melanoma. It was one of the most *benign cancers*, an oxymoron if I've ever heard one. Basal cell cancer is easy to treat, and couldn't have killed me even if it wanted to. 99% of them are simple, small, and never come back. The standard treatment was to scrape them off, or to have a stitch or two in the doctor's office.

That wouldn't cut it for me. Basal cell skin cancer was still cancer. I wanted the big guns. I went to a plastic surgeon and had surgery in a real operating room, with a pathologist waiting to check the tissue before they sewed me up. It was overkill, but worth it for the comfort factor.

I wasn't comfortable for long. Less than a year later, I saw something new in the same spot where the cancer had been taken off. Considering the type of surgery I'd undergone, it was incredibly unlikely that it had come back. Still, worth running by Arnie Klein. And bingo. Not in a good way. So I had one of the first Moh's surgery procedures, now state of the art for skin cancer.

Two cancer surgeries before I was 30—who could blame me for being paranoid?

I'm throwing around terms like *paranoid* not in a clinical sense but in the conversational sense. I have no idea where the lines diverge and where someone crosses over from anxious to

57

phobic. But what lies beneath those other words is a word we all understand: *Fear.* Fear is incredibly human, incredibly humbling, and it had me wrapped tightly in its grip. With the big C at the top of my list, I had no idea how much fear was affecting my behavior, relationships and my life.

Until something lessened my fear and anxiety almost overnight.

Forty-two isn't a big birthday for other people; but for me it was monumental. Forty-two was the age my mom never reached. As it approached, I was clueless about its power and potential. But when I reached forty-two, I felt it in my bones: a sudden shift as the black cloud lifted off me.

Subconsciously I had been expecting to die at forty-one, just as Mom did. Turning forty-two freed me in many ways. Most importantly, it liberated me from fear. I wasn't going to get cancer; I was going to live. This inner transformation was reflected in outward signs. More open, more willing to take risks, more focused on the future, I was also re-evaluating my life.

Some parts of that process proved to be painful, particularly examining a marriage that wasn't working from either partner's perspective. In retrospect, it's not hard to figure out why our whirlwind romance felt so familiar and right. It's also not hard to figure out why it went wrong.

The timing was a tip-off, a sign that I was seeking to repeat the story that shaped me. Obvious as it was, caught up in the romance of romance, I simply didn't see it. I also chose to ignore other signs that were apparent even before the wedding.

I became a cliché the moment I married a man who mirrored so many characteristics of my father. Howard's style in every aspect of his life was to dominate and take control. If the person on the other side resisted, he would wear them down till they gave in. Typically this was a winning strategy in business dealings; and it worked like a charm at home. My lifetime habit was to dutifully go along, and now my sister wasn't around to fight my battles. But as I grew older, became a mother, and developed more trust and confidence in myself and my own opinions, Howard and I grew further apart.

There was one memorable milestone during our marriage when I really stood my ground.

I was about to deliver our second child. After eighteen hours of labor and three hours of pushing, I realized that both my husband and my doctor couldn't take their eyes off the clock in the delivery room.

Obviously we were way past the need to time my contractions. The real action was a few miles away from Cedars Sinai. The Los Angeles Lakers were about to play the final game for the 1988 World Championship. The game was starting at 5:00. I delivered at 4:03, and the delivery room immediately emptied out, as doctors, nurses, even my husband rushed to the nearest TV set.

When the Lakers won the championship, a nurse suggested we name our baby "Magic Johnson." In retrospect, maybe we should have considered it.

We had known for months that we were having a boy, and throughout those months we continually argued about his name.

Howard's current preference was Michael. It wasn't in my top five, but as usual I was starting to cave when we arrived at the hospital for the delivery.

Having spent years across the table from renowned entertainment lawyers and executives on behalf of celebrity clients, Howard was proud of his skill as a negotiator. He knew how to find the jugular and how to zero in to close the deal at the moment of greatest vulnerability.

This occasion offered a textbook moment.

Immediately after I pushed out our almost-10 pound baby, Howard said to me casually, "So it's Michael?" I was too drained to do anything but nod weakly.

The moment Alli first met her new brother.
She wasn't sure she wanted us to keep him. June 1988.

The next morning, 4 year old Alli skipped into my hospital room to meet her new brother. "How's Michael?"

"Not so fast," I said. "He's not going to be Michael."

Alli gave me a look of confusion. Howard gave me a look.

"I was holding him in my arms all night, telling him I love him and I tried to call him Michael but that name wouldn't come out. He's just not a Michael."

Howard was pissed off. "I already ordered the birth certificate."

I shrugged. "I'm sure we can change it."

"To what?"

"I don't know. But not Michael."

We brought Not-Michael home from the hospital with a temporary birth certificate that said Michael. When I walked into the house, there were hilarious signs Howard had created and hung on the walls with various names for our nameless son that made me laugh so hard I almost dropped him. This was classic Howard. He could make me nuts, but he could also make me laugh.

For a week, I held my ground and held our son, calling him "baby" or "sweetheart." The standoff continued. This was the first time I'd stuck to my guns for so long in ten years of marriage.

When our son was eight days old, family and friends arrived at our home for the bris with cards and gifts addressed to "baby boy" or "No-name" or "Generic."

The mohel arrived to perform the ceremony. Ushering Howard and me into a room by ourselves, he took out the certificate to document the fact that our baby boy would be circumcised in the Jewish tradition. He pulled out his pen and smiled at us. "And what is the baby's name?"

Howard and I looked at each other, completely embarrassed. "Can you give us five minutes?"

I guess mohels have seen everything. "Of course." He left the room.

Howard turned to me as soon as we were alone.

"You really want him to be Daniel?" He did have a soft side.

"Yes!" I almost collapsed with relief.

Not so fast. To Howard, this was still a negotiation.

"If you get the name, then I get to choose the new couch for the family room."

A few minutes later, it was a done deal.

I never liked that couch, but it was well worth the trade-off. Our son is definitely a Daniel.

We didn't make it as a couple past his fourth birthday. Our marriage broke up with the chocolate telegram still intact, way in the back of the refrigerator.

Wake Up and Shake Up

The shaking woke me in the middle of the night. Disoriented in the darkness, shock and fear shook me to my senses. I was alone. Separated from Howard, I was living with the kids in our house.

Some primal maternal instinct plus adrenaline propelled me out of bed and down the hall, ignoring the shuddering house and the glass breaking under my bare feet as I ran. I grabbed Daniel out of his bed, carried him to get Alli and brought them both into my room. The kids, even more disoriented than me, were still in their clothes from Disneyland. Howard had taken them there yesterday and brought them home fast asleep last night. I had just arrived home from a business trip a few hours earlier, and hadn't seen them in a week. Sagging with relief, hugging them close, we huddled in my bed. I could practically hear our hearts pounding in the house that was now pitch black, silent, and still.

The morning light exposed broken pieces all over the house—a full wall of mirror shattered in my bathroom, downstairs tiny glass shards that were once our collection of wedding stemware, bottles and dishes that tumbled out of cabinets onto the kitchen floor, broken glass from the family pictures I'd crushed with my bare feet in the hallway while racing to get to the kids. And in the dining room, the loss that stung most. The wooden breakfront had toppled over, crushing my collection of ceramic plates that were cherished memories from trips abroad. I sifted through the pieces, finding a few fragments large enough to possibly be glued together later.

Meanwhile there was no water and a mess to clean up. By the time I got back to the dining room, the broken fragments of ceramics were gone, swept up and tossed out by my cleaning lady who had come to help. The loss of memories was a minor detail in the bigger picture. The Northridge earthquake was the last straw that pushed me out of Los Angeles.

For years I had been wishing we could raise our kids in a smaller community. Howard was always against it. Now that we were no longer together, the universe presented a solution that was both professional and personal.

I had been producing videos and marketing materials for a health-based company located in Monterey. After months of working closely together, despite knowing the pitfalls, I started dating my boss, who owned the company. It evolved into a serious relationship, which allowed me to avoid the singles scene in my forties.

Having a long distance relationship felt familiar and easy. I kept my home and love lives separate; seeing V only on weekends when I didn't have my kids. Occasional trips to visit him in Carmel made living in a small town feel more real. So what happened after the Northridge earthquake wasn't entirely shocking. When the earth moved in LA, it moved me, too. Exactly six months from the date of the earthquake, I married V and moved with the kids to Carmel.

The Wedding Curse

I never thought I'd be the type to get married twice. Not that anyone else does. Still, lots of us do marry again, and we do it with the same hopes and dreams we bring to the first one.

After my first wedding, I had a whole list of things I would have done differently. Dumb and dumber? Repeating some of them the second time. When asked if I wanted a diamond engagement ring, I said no, thank you. Twice. Both weddings involved long distance moves, but both were rushed and took place within weeks of the decision to get married. This meant a rerun of the same problems—like planning the wedding.

This must sound unthinkable to brides who spend over a year arranging and executing every detail so they can have the event of their dreams. Both of my weddings were far from perfect. Both took place in one of our parents' homes, and both were pretty much slapped together by someone else. Marrying V, I had only a few weeks to uproot my home, move, start the kids in a new school, and get married. All while working fulltime. Who had time to choose flowers, food, music, cake, or even a dress?

Although the event took place in her home, V's mother was sick the day of our wedding and wasn't even there...which kind of balanced my side of the aisle. My father, raised Orthodox, could not accept me marrying a non-Jew. A few weeks before the wedding, he flew out to Los Angeles from Florida on a last minute mission to change my mind, bringing a book titled *How to Stop an Inter-marriage*, apparently aimed at an audience of 20-somethings. I was 44, not planning to have more children, and the kids I had were already purebred Jewish.

The story would have made an amusing episode of *Curb Your Enthusiasm*, only this was my life. Dad was my only parent, my rock and role model, and I had always taken pride in being a good daughter. I begged and pleaded with him until the last minute, but he refused to attend our wedding. Even more unthinkable, after the wedding, he refused to speak to me at all. The good daughter had turned into the black sheep.

My relationship with my dad formed the firmament, the foundation of my life, the bedrock I stood upon. My trust, confidence and admiration of him were absolute. I could not take in or process his withdrawal from my life. This was not some run of the mill family dispute. This was a seismic shake up at the highest level of the family Richter scale, a broken piece that pierced me to my core.

You'd think that was drama enough. But there was another confounding problem surrounding the wedding: karma.

We had a narrow window of time before my kids would start their new school in Carmel, so we selected the date of July 17. Hoping to persuade my father to come, I started calling around to find a rabbi who would marry us. I was moving to a one-temple town, so I wasn't that surprised when the rabbi turned me down. Further research turned up a "freelance" rabbi, who said she was willing to marry me to a non-Jew.

Until I told her the date.

There was a long pause over the phone. Then she told me that according to that year's Jewish calendar, I had picked a particularly ill-omened date—a disastrous day in history for Jews. She refused to marry us on that day, she insisted that no other rabbi would marry us that day, and she warned me: *do not get married on July 17.*

Oy vey.

What can I say? Love is blind. It's also deaf.

Switching the date proved to be a logistical problem for my brother and sister coming from the east coast. Not superstitious and obviously not Jewish, V assured me that he was not worried about the date and I shouldn't worry either. About to marry a WASP with a super stiff upper lip, I was proud of myself for stiffening up my own lip. I can't blame anyone but myself for throwing the rabbi's warning to the winds and going forward with the plans.

We got married on July 17 by a local judge. It was freezing cold and drizzly, but lightning didn't strike anyone dead. We were married, life went on, and I forgot about the ill omen of our wedding date…until one year later, when July 17 rolled around again.

The traditional first year anniversary gift is *paper.* Appropriately, that's what I got on our first anniversary, only it didn't come from my husband. The paper came from my breast surgeon, who handed me the pathology report from my mastectomy a few days earlier, with a terrifying prognosis.

That's when I remembered the rabbi and her warning about the date.

I could chalk it up to coincidence if the bad karma ended there. But the first few years of our union brought a string of other problems—ill omens kept coming like a broken record from the universe. The business went under. The cat unexpectedly died. V's assistant embezzled our money.

I started believing our run of bad luck was not a coincidence. Every time something bad happened, I replayed the rabbi's warning over and over in my head, repeating my litany to my no-longer-new husband. "I should have listened. God is punishing us." It was getting kind of hard to celebrate every July 17.

I'm not religious, but I was reeling. I couldn't shake the feeling that a curse was hanging over our marriage. I felt helpless, powerless, a victim of the universe.

If I've learned anything from cancer, it's the importance of NOT feeling helpless, NOT feeling like a victim, and NOT ignoring my own gut. I felt I needed to listen, to adapt, and somehow take control. "I don't want to go through our lives with this curse hanging over our heads."

By now V was a believer. "So what do we do?"

"We get married again. On a different date."

We had just moved to our third home in eight years of marriage. It felt like the right time for a fresh start. This time I officially checked out the Hebrew calendar first. We settled on a date, then settled on the couch in our new home to say our own short simple vows, all by ourselves. No guests, no rabbi, no fuss, no party (though I did eat some chocolate to celebrate.)

That was it. It wasn't wildly romantic, but it was symbolic. It was July 25 and it felt right. We couldn't wipe out the past, but we wiped out the date. I even stopped wearing my wedding band with the old date inscribed.

Attempting to defy our negative karma proved to me that the human mind is a powerful force. That simple act of changing our wedding date had an unexpected power: completely changing my mindset somehow completely changed our luck. Our run of bad things stopped happening once we re-dated our anniversary.

Now when July 17 comes up on the calendar, I don't even notice it. I'm satisfied to celebrate the new date, and to know that even if I picked the wrong day, at least I picked the right person.

Family Functions

Along with the good things about V came one thorny little detail: like me, born of two New York Jews, V also is a product of his background, the flip side of mine: translated, I married a conservative Republican.

I never signed up for this, of course. I might have been more likely to marry an axe murderer. Although I'm sure some axe murderers have very nice qualities—as I discovered some Republicans do.

The nice qualities are what allowed me to overlook the Republican issue when V and I got married. I had come out of a marriage to a Democrat, who began voting Republican towards the end of the marriage. I'm not saying it caused our divorce, but it sure didn't help. So since I'd already been married to a covert Republican, it didn't seem like a huge leap to marry another one.

Early on, while dealing with blended families and a life-threatening illness, party politics didn't loom large over the marital bed. Once the drama dropped down, we settled into a Mary Matalin/James Carville kind of life. V's family and friends knew about my blue blood, but in their presence, I tried to keep my outrage to a low simmer. V's party affiliation was never a problem with my side. My family and friends are far more opinionated and vocal, and V can barely get a word in no matter what we're talking about. If he wore his Republican heart on his sleeve, he would have his sleeve torn off.

So I was blue, he was red; we never became purple. We canceled out each other's votes and avoided intense political discussions. My main strategy consisted of diversionary tactics—inventing errands for V on Election Day, or distracting him so he would forget to go to the polls.

Politics was only one of our differences. He's a WASP, I'm Jewish. He's a morning person; I'm a night owl. I blurt out whatever I'm thinking. V is a "still waters run deep" kind of guy. And often I never know what's below those still waters.

Another difference is that he's really low key and I'm more of a drama queen. I might announce as I walk in the door, "Guess what! Something amazing happened! I won five dollars in the lottery!" Whereas V is the kind of person who would look up in the middle of dinner and say calmly, "Oh, I forgot to tell you. I won the Nobel prize two days ago."

So it was entirely in keeping with our characters that a few years ago, I opened the mail one day and noticed one of those Democratic Party appeals for money. But the name at the top wasn't mine. It was V's. Which is how I learned that my Republican husband was now a registered Democrat.

V proved adaptable personally as well as politically. In fact, both of my husbands were adaptable, adjusting to our "new normal." Although friendly divorces are more common now, people were often surprised by our family dynamic.

From day one, Howard was an integral part of our new blended family, staying in our new home with the kids while V and I went on a three day honeymoon. At Daniel's weekend sports games, the other parents never knew which of my two husbands might show up with me. Sometimes both. It was a win/win for everyone, especially the kids.

The smoothness and congeniality of our triangle was due to V and Howard, who appreciated and respected each other's roles and never crossed the lines. V was willing to include Howard in every family event or occasion; and Howard honored that on his side, even sending V and me cards on our anniversary every year. Although they were polar opposites in some ways, from the beginning they bonded over the kids, sports, and playing golf together. And they found areas of common ground: somehow, sloppy and disorganized as I am, I managed to marry a neat freak, not once but twice.

Most importantly, both husbands lived up to the priority I lived by: the kids come first. As most divorcing couples discover, no marriage can fully be over when you share children. Feelings remain and evolve, and friendship can, too. I can't say Howard and I never had our differences or disagreements, but I can say we remained a parenting partnership, with our children as the focus.

My mothering style was very hands-on, a graceful way to describe a mother with a healthy amount of anxiety, intense separation issues, and difficulty letting her kids out of her personal zone of control. (Note to self: separation and lack of control are impossible to avoid when you get divorced.)

The year I remarried, already filled with angst and guilt for moving my kids away from their dad, I first started sending them on flights to Los Angeles to visit Howard. The kids were six and ten, and I don't think flying alone was very hard for them but it was agony for me.

This was before 9/11 so I was allowed to accompany them to the gate at the San Jose airport. They wore little tags from the airline for kids flying alone, which made them feel proud but made me feel guilty. I was definitely capable of chasing them down the jetway, flinging myself at them in tears. (I'm fairly certain that scene played out only in my imagination.)

I'd stand at the entrance to the jetway and reluctantly let them go after they allowed me to smother them with as many hugs and kisses as they could tolerate in public. Walking down the tunnel together, they seemed fragile and vulnerable under heavy huge backpacks which dwarfed their small bodies. At six, Daniel instinctively understood that I needed him to look back at me before he disappeared from my sight. He always did.

Then they would vanish into the plane and I could let the tears go. While the other passengers boarded, I'd stand at the window sobbing, wondering where the kids were sitting. When the plane backed away, I'd stay at the gate, jealous of all the intact families traveling with their kids, while I would be returning to an empty house.

I always waited until I knew their plane was in the air before walking back to the car. I won't even go into scenarios I would imagine, about what could happen between the time the plane rolled away from the gate and the moment their father would meet them at the other end.

It turned out my angst actually had a benefit. Learning how to let go and let my kids fly alone turned out to be a valuable and important step for later, when circumstances forced me to let go of control and let go of my kids in lots of ways. This lesson wasn't just for me, but more importantly, for them. Maybe I'm trying to see a negative aspect of divorce in a positive light, but I think flying alone helped prepare my kids for stormier skies ahead.

Left to my own devices, I would have over-coddled and over-comforted them. I would have avoided the slightest tinge of suffering. Divorce taught them that life includes bumps; and they took baby steps in resilience and adaptability. Those small steps helped give them the confidence and independence to know they could take bigger steps without me standing right there. And I needed to know that, too.

A Full Plate

Transplanted from the Westside of Los Angeles to the small scenic town of Carmel on the central California coast, my kids and I were three fish out of water. Partly in a good way. Taking them to afterschool activities used to put us in bumper to bumper freeway traffic. Now we could walk a few blocks and be at the beach. In Los Angeles, I would warn Alli not to open the door unless the burglar alarm was turned off. In Carmel, she wondered why we never used our alarm system and why V routinely left his car unlocked in the driveway with his wallet and keys in it.

Still, even in paradise, life felt somewhat short of idyllic. I was a typical working mom, overstretched and overburdened, working on V's startup business that looked like it would never get started. Trying to ignore my loneliness for friends left behind in Los Angeles, I yearned for more connection in my new community. Hoping to preserve the passion in a new marriage, I patched together a new family unit. Coping with children suffering the aftershocks of our move, I ignored the heartbreak from the break with my dad.

I had a full plate.

It took an entire school year for me to rearrange the broken pieces enough to feel settled, and satisfied enough to look ahead rather than back.

Daniel was turning seven, and I had planned the ultimate boy's birthday party. At a nearby park, we would spread out an enormous plastic ground cover and Daniel's friends would fling at each other an array of the messiest, gooiest edibles we could come up with: yogurt, whipped cream, spaghetti, chocolate pudding. The kids couldn't wait for the food fight fantasy.

About a week before the party I was in the shower when I felt a little bump under my armpit. For a cancer phobe like me, my reaction demonstrates how liberated I was from fear: I passed right over the bump without giving it a second thought.

I didn't remember it a few days later in the shower as I slid my soapy hands around my right breast and thought it felt kind of lumpy. I wasn't too concerned. Thanks to my documentary research and reading, I knew that breast cancer typically presented itself as a hard little lump in one spot. What I felt was nothing like that.

There was something about the size of a giant gumball, plus lumpy sections in other parts of the breast. My yearly mammogram had been eight months ago and my obsessive fear of cancer had nearly disappeared. Besides, breasts were not even on my top five list of body parts that I worried about as cancer targets.

I got dressed and went in to work. During a break that morning, I called the local mammography center.

"Who is your doctor, ma'am.?" The receptionist asked.

"I don't have a doctor. I felt a lump and I want a mammogram."

"I'm sorry, but a mammogram can only be ordered by a doctor."

"I just moved here and I didn't need a doctor till now. Can't you just give me a mammogram?"

She would not be moved.

I could have dropped it there and waited, but being turned down bugged me. So I called the only local doctor I knew well enough to ask for a favor. Scott Kantor was an orthopedic surgeon, the father of Daniel's classmate, who lived a few doors down the street. He arranged for a mammogram the next Monday. That weekend, his son Josh was one of the goopy guests at the infamous food fight celebrating Daniel's 7th birthday.

Mothers know that feeling of special satisfaction when we've done something we know our kids appreciate. That's the feeling I savored Monday while my breast was smashed, flattened and mammogrammed. I didn't even feel my medical antennae go up when the tech came in to do a second picture. I got dressed, went home, made dinner, and was exercising on our HealthRider, singing along to a videotape of *Oklahoma*, when the doorbell rang at 9 p.m.

It was Dr. Scott Kantor. Now my medical antennae went up. Way up.

V joined us in the family room. I sat on the edge of the couch, every nerve and fiber in my body on high alert. There was an eerie simultaneous sense of detachment, as if I was watching a movie I wanted to leap up and stop. I felt misplaced, in our one-year rental on a flowered couch that didn't even belong to us. This couldn't be my life.

Scott had brought my mammograms along. As an orthopedic surgeon, he knew nothing about breast cancer, so the chief radiologist had spent the last few hours giving Scott a crash course. He had learned enough to communicate the very strong probability that those little white dots V and I could see on the picture of my breast were likely malignant.

Scott is an excellent doctor and a genuinely good guy. Thinking he was just doing a simple favor, instead he ended up with the job of delivering horrible news. He urged me to get a biopsy as soon as possible.

He was preaching to the choir. With even a hint of cancer, "as soon as possible" meant *now*. My whole medical support system was in Los Angeles, carefully curated after years of anticipating cancer. At the top of my list was Dr. Philip Brooks, a prominent gynecologist and good friend who had delivered Alli. I called him at home the minute Scott Kantor walked out the door. Hearing the panic in my voice, Philip responded by moving mountains at Cedars Sinai to arrange for a one-day blitz. The next day, V and I made plans to fly down to Los Angeles.

Even that wasn't simple. Moving, work, and a new marriage had meant no time to develop connections in our new community. During the school year, I had patched together high school babysitters to get me through the days at work, but my local support system was so limited, I had no one to babysit for more than a few hours. In a strange twist on my own history, I called Aunt Helen's daughter Abbey, who came down from San Francisco to watch my kids for the day.

A further complication was the date. This was happening the week of July 4. For me Independence Day is all broken pieces. My mother died on July 4th. That's also the date Howard moved out of the house. In a few years, my father would die that same weekend.

Not that there is ever a good time to get cancer, but the timing sucked.

Straight from the airport, I went into a round of diagnostic mammograms at Cedars Sinai, then V and I carried my test results over to the surgeon's office in the building next door. I was in a fog. But one thing stood out in sharp focus: stains on the waiting room carpet. It's one thing for me to be messy, but my surgeon should be meticulous.

I had a strong impulse to walk out. I had the same impulse a few hours later, when I was in a gown, on a gurney, about to be wheeled into the operating room. As I met the anesthesiologist about to put me under, my immediate negative reaction was similar to what I felt when I met the surgeon. Hyper-sensitive, with my mother's misdiagnosis at the very top of my mind, I was not only fearful but I also felt both of them were condescending when they talked to me. It rubbed me the wrong way.

"Get off the gurney and get out of here," my inner voice advised.

"Shut up," my brain responded. "Do you have any idea how hard it was to get this appointment and schedule this surgery so fast?"

Shoving down the fear that something would go wrong, I forced my body to stay on the gurney. My rational mind was pleading to just get this biopsy over with, while my inner voices were shouting so loud I couldn't think straight. It was a relief when they finally put the mask over my face and put me out.

I woke up in recovery, got bandaged up, then flew home. While waiting days for the results, all I wanted to do was to hold my children close. But I had to dodge hugs since I was sore and I hadn't told them about the biopsy.

Almost a week later, the surgeon called with the biopsy report. I sank onto our bed, with V across from me on the other line. What I didn't know until V told me several years later moved this surgeon up even higher on my shit list. He had walked out of the operating room and told V, privately and confidentially, what he saw inside my breast. Like a scene out of *Mad Men*, or maybe my own mother's experience, my husband already knew the news my doctor was about to deliver.

The lump was malignant. Cancer had spread beyond the lump, throughout my breast. A mastectomy was my only option. There was no way, the doctor told me with gravity over the phone from Los Angeles, to "save my breast."

"Save my breast?" I almost snorted. It never occurred to me that sparing my breast would be a priority. I didn't give a shit about my breast at that moment, or any other moment since I had talked to Scott Kantor. What I wanted to hear was about *saving* something else. I sat on my bed and tried to digest the fact that I was going to die.

Cancer World

When the doctor told me I had cancer I left the bed where I was sitting, left the room, left my life. I continued talking to the doctor, I talked to V after I hung up, and I went through the motions of living. But I wasn't there. I was in Cancer World— suddenly and profoundly alone.

Despite all these years and all I know, describing how it feels to have cancer is like trying to describe to a man what it's like to have a baby. Even if that man is a doctor and has gone to medical school and delivered hundreds of babies, there's no way he can ever really know what it feels like to have a human being grow in your body for nine months, how it feels when it moves around inside and what you experience as it shoves itself down through your innards, struggling to come out. You look at this living, breathing, crying, slimy, exquisite, magical thing that just emerged from you and could never have existed on this planet without your nourishment and your body and then you hold it in your arms and there's no way anyone who has a penis can comprehend the whole constellation of the pain and ecstasy that is childbirth.

Having cancer is something like that, something no one else can really describe to someone who has not had it, no matter how much they have studied cancer—even studied cancer and won a Nobel Prize. No matter how much they love you, support you, come to every single appointment, live through your treatment, dry your tears and hold your hand, there is no way a cancer-free person can get what it's like to live inside Cancer World.

Not that Cancer World is the same for everyone. It depends on your diagnosis and prognosis. If your case is treatable and not life threatening, you can float through Cancer World like visiting the dentist and going right home. For others, it's like stepping into quicksand that sucks you in and you can't get out. Finding out you could die definitely puts you across the threshold.

I was flung into Cancer World. After becoming a fulltime resident, I figured out the source of the permanent shadow that hovers over everyone who lives there. *I felt like a victim.*

Nothing drains your mojo faster than putting on a hospital gown. Everything about the circumstances surrounding cancer expands on that, making you feel out of control and completely helpless. You lose faith and trust in your own body. You have no idea why this evil thing chose your body as the place to spread its deadly tentacles. Worst of all, you have absolutely no way to know, nor do your doctors, how to make it go away.

Here it was. My worst nightmare. My deepest, blackest fear was back with a bullet. The shit hit the fan. The shit was all over the room.

It felt both impossible and inevitable.

I knew I was going to die. But not yet. First I needed to get the breast off, and I wasn't going back to that surgeon. So step one was to find the right surgeon.

You know what? Let me back up a little. The calm logic of that sentence bears no resemblance to what was really going on.

Instead of saying "Step one was to find the right surgeon," this is closer to what I would have written back then:

HOLY SHIT. THE LUMP WASN'T THERE WHEN I HAD A MAMMOGRAM EIGHT MONTHS AGO, SO THIS CANCER MUST BE GROWING LIKE GANGBUSTERS. I NEED SOMEONE TO CUT THIS FUCKING THING OUT OF ME RIGHT NOW!!!!&#*&

That sounds a little more realistic.

I was a good girl who'd followed the rules in every area of life—a compliant wife, employee, daughter, sister, friend. But due to my mom's death, in medicine I played by different rules. I wasn't the type of patient who calls to make an appointment and the receptionist in the surgeon's office tells you that his schedule is very busy but he can see you for a consultation three weeks from Friday, the patient says okay and takes the appointment. That wasn't me.

I was convinced I had the mother of all cancers and I had NO time to waste since every day I was getting closer to dying from that cancer and I needed it out of my body RIGHT THIS MINUTE. Apparently, I managed to communicate that urgency because the very next week I returned to Los Angeles and had the mastectomy exactly one week after the biopsy. (Even though the doctor's receptionist had told me that would be impossible.)

No denying, at times I was a difficult, demanding patient. I did whatever I thought would help me advocate for myself. Resources and respect for patients' wishes and needs were not as prevalent in 1995. It's far different than today, when the doctor/patient relationship is more of a partnership.

My mother's experience also affected my approach. If I intended to avoid her fate, I believed being accommodating and accepting was not an option.

Difficult as it was, arranging for a mastectomy long distance without consulting first with the surgeon proved to be the simpler part of scheduling the surgery. There was a major complication involving my travel to Los Angeles. (Of course there was. In my world, *everything* is complicated.)

Eight weeks of camp every summer was my favorite part of childhood, and I had eagerly awaited the day I would send my own kids off to camp. With the universe displaying incredibly inconvenient timing, that day was here. At eleven, Alli was going to camp for two weeks for the first time. I couldn't wait for her to experience camp the same way I did.

Eleven years as a mother, and I still had not fully grasped some of the basic truths of parenting, which are also basic truths of life. You can't make life work a certain way for your children just because you want it to.

Many, if not most, parents make the same mistake. We want our children's lives to be perfect. We want them to have what we had. Or we don't want them to have what we had. No matter what we want, or don't want, or think we want, we get what we get. I hadn't fully absorbed that yet. Although I had just been diagnosed with cancer, I could not let go of my plan to send my child off to have the camp experience of her dreams (which of course were really *my* dreams).

What sounds like a relatively simple and solvable problem actually contained two major issues. One was my anxiety over my children and my need to control everything about their lives as much as possible so everything would be as perfect as possible. The concept of someone else organizing Alli's clothes and her items for camp, someone else packing her trunk, and worst of all, someone else actually TAKING her to camp and leaving her there other than me, well, that just couldn't happen.

The other issue was worse. I had to make an impossible decision between two choices, both unacceptable. One option was telling Alli the truth: that I was going to LA to have a mastectomy. That meant she either would insist on staying home or go away to camp knowing that her mother had cancer. I knew Alli would choose to stay home, which meant she would miss out on what I considered one of life's *best* childhood experiences. Instead, she would have one of life's *worst* childhood experiences.

My other option was to lie. I could send Alli off to camp and tell her about my cancer when she came home. That second course seemed simpler, but for me was far more complex.

Lying to my children wouldn't have been so tragic but it happened to be the worst part of my own history repeating itself. My parents sent me off to camp withholding the information that my mother had cancer, a decision that had tormented me my entire life. I could *never* do the exact same thing to my own daughter.

Which proves that we should never say *never*. After agonizing over it, I decided that Alli did not need to know the truth...yet. That way we would both be able to do what we most needed to do during those two weeks. For the first time ever, rather than taking care of my children, my own needs had to come first. I

85

told the kids that V and I had business in Los Angeles that was very, very important. So important that I would miss Alli's departure. Her dad would come up and take her to camp instead.

The kids bought the story, and I have to confess that lying was easier than I expected. Far more difficult was thinking about telling them the truth. For the first time I understood some of the agony my mother must have felt.

How would I ever manage to look in my children's eyes and take away the security of their childhoods? How would I find the strength to hold them up when the whole world was collapsing?

I couldn't bear to imagine them growing up without their mom. And that wasn't the ultimate horror in my imagination. I had lived it. I believed history was repeating itself and I projected my past onto my kids. Alli was me—older, resilient, tougher. Daniel was my brother Josh—the baby, more vulnerable to the loss of a mother. Even more horrifying, he was far younger than Josh had been. How could Daniel ever recover?

Their innocence stabbed me in the heart right under my cancerous breast. Saying goodbye to my children on the eve of my mastectomy elevated my emotional stress beyond what I thought I could endure. Not for one instant was I worried about losing my breast. I was consumed with losing my life, and my children losing me. Distraught, drained, depressed, I was alone in Cancer World tormented by my dark destiny.

Out of Control

Prior to a mastectomy, many women find ways to bid farewell to the breast they're about to lose—they light candles, soak in luxurious baths, take boudoir pictures. I did nothing like that. I felt no warm feelings, no lingering sadness at saying goodbye. I couldn't wait to get the damn thing out of my life.

This time, there were no stains on the carpet. I had full confidence and trust in Dr. Armando Guiliano, one of the nation's leading breast surgeons.

The surgery was on my body, but it was an out-of-body experience. It didn't feel real. This was happening to someone else, like it wasn't me on the operating table. Not me waking up with a bandage wrapped around my chest where my right breast used to be. Not me lying in a hospital room far from home and my children. Not me who did not want to see, call, or even communicate with anyone I knew. Someone else was living in Cancer World.

V and I had to spend a few days in Los Angeles while I recovered from surgery. So there we were, in the perfect place for a couple on their first anniversary, a luxury hotel without the kids around. Room service. Relaxation. Romance. Except we could have done without the bandages and two drains coming out of my body.

At the time I had no comprehension or concern for things over on V's side. Completely immersed in my own pain, I never noticed his. He took it all in: my confusion, complaints, frustrations, fears. I was queasier about my own body than he was. He changed my bandages and drainage bottles. I depended on his physical presence—it comforted me to feel his skin, his solidity, his strength. He listened. Instinctively he knew how to be supportive without patronizing or pitying me. If things were reversed, I could never have matched his devotion.

And he never complained. Sure, he was a WASP with a stiff upper lip. Still, this was not what he signed up for, spending our first anniversary in Dr. Guiliano's office getting the results of my pathology report.

I didn't need a translation from scientific jargon to the English language to recognize the results as very very bad news: Stage III with complications far worse than I expected. I was hearing a death sentence, screaming inside while trying to absorb what lay ahead.

Back in Carmel, recovering from surgery and digesting my diagnosis, the next step was to decide on a treatment plan. Like everything else in Cancer World, that sounded so much simpler than it would prove to be. Immediately, one thing became clear: my situation was the opposite of clear. With a highly complicated case, debated by the hospital tumor board, it wouldn't be smart to follow the recommendation of my doctor without seeking second, third, and maybe more opinions.

The ideal situation is to find an oncologist you trust, and make your treatment decisions as a team. This team approach wasn't embraced by many doctors at the time. Yet whether my doctor liked it or not, I needed to be an active participant in my healthcare. Fearing that I would repeat my mother's destiny and die due to a doctor's mistake made me hyper-vigilant, hyper-paranoid, hyper- everything. That meant searching beyond my doctor's suggestions by doing my own independent research.

I knew how to do research, how to amass and process information, evaluate and extract the essentials. Only choosing a cancer treatment wasn't comparable to a term paper or TV show where your success is determined by higher grades or higher ratings. With your life at stake, you feel *desperate* to make the best, most informed decision.

I went into ultra-high gear, immersed myself in reading and investigating every option. The internet was in its infancy; there was not much information or support to be found online. So I called everyone I knew who knew anyone with contacts in the cancer community. I called doctors around the country, consulted with top cancer centers. My brother Josh, an ear, nose and throat doctor, managed to arrange a phone consult I desperately wanted with a top doctor at Sloan-Kettering. That short conversation was pivotal in finding peace with my ultimate decision.

Everyone agreed that in addition to the surgery, I needed radiation and chemotherapy, but I got different treatment recommendations in each place.

That's not what any patient wants to hear. Uncertainty is one of the most stressful aspects of any challenge. Years ago I heard about a study illustrating that. A group of soldiers were given ultra-heavy backpacks and told they were going on a long march. One half of the group was told they were expected to march 50 miles; the other half was simply told to start marching and not told the distance they were expected to complete. Result? 100% of the first group completed 50 miles. Only 60% of the second group completed the full 50 miles. As long as you know what you are facing, you can accomplish it.

There's the catch-22. It's hard to steel yourself to face a challenge until you know what it is. Choosing cancer treatment can be a tough choice, especially for a civilian. When you do the research, the more you read, the more you learn there is to read. There is so much more to read than you can ever learn.

For me, the bigger problem was that the more I learned, the more I realized there were not going to be any right answers. This is a really difficult concept for someone who prided herself on being a good student and getting good grades. Cancer is the biggest test of your life—and often there are no right answers. That also applies to a lot of other challenges in life. There aren't necessarily answers that are one-size-fits-all. There is however, an answer that suits each individual. The trick is finding the answer which best fits *you*.

And the trickiest part is finding the answers that aren't in your head, but in your gut. We're accustomed to respond to our thoughts, our own ideas plus the thoughts and words of people who influence us. Our minds can easily drown out quieter truths buried deeper inside. Probably I'd been getting signals from my gut for many years, but I was just learning how to listen and trust them. It was like adjusting a radio dial to hear a distant broadcast while attempting to tune out the static.

This meant I had to adopt a new practice, to venture outside my comfort zone. I almost always did what I was expected to do. I had lived nearly my entire life connected to a controlling father or a controlling husband, and my gut feelings didn't play a key role in those partnerships. Now I was divorced from Howard. My father wasn't speaking to me. V was the opposite of controlling. My former pattern was out the window.

Plus I was in Cancer World, profoundly alone. Nothing I had ever known had such potential to make me more frightened; and nothing had such potential to make me more fierce.

V and I flew down to LA for a consultation at a prestigious medical center. We had waited a couple weeks to get an appointment, waited more than an hour in the waiting room, and another half hour wait in a small examining room. All the waiting fit, because I was a patient. Only I was the opposite of *patient*. Who invented that term, anyway? Who can be patient when everything in you is screaming URGENT!

But I didn't scream anything. I waited impatiently, while my brain reeled. Not just from having cancer that could leave my kids motherless. I was also reeling from trying to figure out the options and odds. With one protocol, someone with my particular profile and pathology had a 30% chance of being alive in 10 years. With another protocol, the survival percentage went up 2% but there was a 10 percent increased possibility the treatment itself could kill me. How do you calculate those odds?

During my first pregnancy, I was so neurotic I kept daily track of survival percentages in case of a premature birth. I could have told you on any given day, if Alli had been born, what were the odds that she would survive.

Now I was calculating odds based on Daniel's age. If I lived five years, he would be 12 when I died; if I lived ten years he would be 17. This went on in my brain all day long. (Oddly enough, I don't enjoy Las Vegas.)

So I calculated, and I waited. And finally the doctor came in.

I like it when men are clear and strong and decisive, which he was. But that's all I liked. Let's not even mention the fact that he was condescending. The gist of his message was that to avoid inevitable doom, I should check into the medical center immediately and have a bone marrow transplant. For several weeks I would be confined to a sterile room with no human contact. There was a decent chance the treatment could kill me but assuming it didn't, they'd send me home afterwards and hope my cancer didn't come back.

Too new to have solid scientific data behind it, ultra-high dose chemotherapy was the latest research being touted for breast cancer at the time, and I fit the criteria for this trial. Since my diagnosis, I had been saying that I wanted the most aggressive treatment possible, everything science had to offer. This was it.

Sitting in that exam room, suddenly a vision of myself in that sterile hospital room popped into my head, with a matching feeling deep in my gut. And in that instant something became crystal clear: a bone marrow transplant was not the answer for me.

I said nothing as the doctor continued. He would make a call to arrange a tour of the unit right now and could get me admitted into the program immediately.

When he left the room, V turned to me, "What do you think?"

I didn't think. I didn't need to. I got up, walked out of the exam room, down the hall and out of the building. I never looked back.

I don't recommend that anyone repeat this move. Hopefully you can come up with a more socially appropriate way to communicate with a doctor. My behavior was just plain rude. But at that moment, it felt right. Deep down in my bones kind of right. My inner signals had been simmering since I saw the stain on the surgeon's carpet. Now they boiled over. This was my personal tipping point, time to listen to my gut, time to trust it. Time to take control of my own cancer journey and my own life.

The Decider

After weighing all the advice and information I collected, I chose the chemo protocol my oncologist had first recommended. It was categorized as high dose, more toxic and stringent than those used today, and offered my best odds for survival. Called the Milan Sequential Protocol, almost a full year of treatment, this regimen projected a 38% chance of being alive in ten years, without a relapse.

Since those numbers didn't inspire confidence, I continued my desperate search for something to tip the percentage in my favor. Calculating odds like a bookie, struggling to read scientific studies with Latin words and medical terms I didn't understand, I spent every waking hour researching and reading about cancer.

About a week after my first chemo infusion, I read about something that no doctor had suggested. It was rarely done in the U.S., but this option spoke to me. Loudly. In Europe, to treat estrogen-positive cancer like I had, women often had their ovaries removed.

I would have taken off my right arm to see my kids graduate high school. I called my oncologist in Los Angeles.

"No way. It's overkill." He was firm. "And I can't allow you to have surgery in the middle of heavy duty chemo."

I trusted him. I liked him. I was programmed to listen to him. But days went by, and I still had a nagging feeling about those ovaries. The feeling would not go away.

I asked him again, then asked a few other doctors, who agreed with my oncologist. (Today things have changed; removing ovaries is commonly done, although not during chemo.) Up against the doctors' collective decades of study and experience, the sum total of my medical knowledge was zero. I knew nothing about hormones and how they affect the growth of cancer cells. I knew only that something was telling me to take out my ovaries and I could not let it go.

Could I even think of going against my doctor's advice at a time when my life was at stake? Did I have the guts to go with my gut?

After a week of paralyzing indecision and inner turmoil, I made a decision and the bigger decision behind it. Like my rejection of high dose chemo, this would prove, in the years to come, to be the right choice for me. I called Philip Brooks, who was a pioneer in laparoscopic surgery. Surgery during chemotherapy was a controversial choice; his support and understanding were my lifeline.

"I think it's unnecessary, but if this is important to you, let's do it."

My former next-door neighbor, an anesthesiologist at Cedars Sinai, agreed to be there, too. "You'll come through this fine," he assured me.

My confidence in them was buoyed by their confidence in me. As the patient, I wanted a voice in my own health, to help make my own choices. It seemed so basic, so sensible. I didn't realize how revolutionary this concept was, or that patient advocacy would become so acceptable and accepted in the years to come. Back then, all I knew is that my conscience allowed no other choice. I could, and would find a new oncologist. My decision to take out my ovaries at that point meant that essentially I became the captain of my life journey.

A Fair to Remember

Often forced to be MIA as a mom during cancer treatment, I was determined to keep my kids' lives as normal as possible. At least as close as I could manage to anything resembling normal. Soon after I started chemo, I spent a day with Alli and Daniel at the Monterey County fair.

The previous year we had just moved to the area, and we had spent hours walking around, meeting farm animals, going on rides, eating funnel cakes and cotton candy till we couldn't breathe. Having cancer at the fair, I felt like a feeble shadow of my former self. Weakened and mildly nauseous, I went only on the carousel, ate only white rice and water, and spent much of the day sitting on a bench resting. I felt cursed, out-of-sync with life, robbed of youth and spirit as if someone had sucked all the fun out of me.

Even more, I hated that the kids felt the same way. Recently Daniel had told me his "real mom" had long hair and was nicer. Alli confided that she mentally referred to the current version of me as "the cancer mom."

No surprise, I also felt like "the cancer wife." At the fair, I watched V sitting on a bench while the kids and I rode the carousel. Unaware I could see him, he looked sad, depressed, in pain. It hurt me to see, and to think what an effort it must be for him to be upbeat around me when he must feel so overloaded and burdened. I hated what I had become.

After a few hours, V and I took Daniel home, while Alli stayed at the fair with a friend and her family. When they dropped her off later, she came in to say goodnight, radiant after having a fabulous time. Though it hurt that I hadn't been able to share the experience, I felt happy to see her so happy. Poignantly, it reminded me of the night I came home from college and found my tired, sick Mom in bed. All I was missing was the bed jacket.

Hair Today, Gone Tomorrow

That bump under my armpit, the clue I didn't read at first, was a red flag early on that my cancer had spread beyond the breast to my lymph nodes. So since the beginning, I knew I needed chemo, and knew I would lose my thick, wavy, waist-length hair. Preoccupied with my own impending hair loss, I was also occupied with the hair on my kids' heads. In the weeks before I got cancer, they had their own hair drama going on.

The drama came from two little words that are any parent's nightmare: Head. Lice. Or is it one word? Headlice? Either way, I don't have to describe the fear and loathing.

Today you can actually *hire* people to come to your home and deal with this. At the time, professional head lice hunters hadn't been invented as a job description, so the task fell to me. I did everything humanly possible but the bugs had evolved beyond the capabilities of human doggedness. Trying to get rid of them was infuriating and irritating and incredibly laborious. I would stand there combing Alli's long thick hair strand by strand with the lice comb, trying to keep a fun attitude for her sake while dreading that I would get it, too.

Naturally, I did. And not long afterwards, when I got diagnosed with cancer, I remember thinking: "Perfect. I finally found the cure for head lice: chemotherapy."

I'm in awe of those brave women who buzz off the hair before it falls out. More wimp than warrior, I dreaded being bald and wanted to hang onto every hair I had for as long as I could. I harbored fantasies that I could save at least some of it—and trust me, I tried. But the products, potions, and prayers didn't pan out.

A couple weeks after my first chemo infusion, hair started falling out all over the place—in strands, locks, and handfuls; and my hairline started receding all around from the outside in. The texture changed, too: it looked and felt less like hair and more like straw. Pretty soon what remained was only tenuously attached to the top of my head. I was so desperate to keep any of it that I stopped brushing, washing, or even touching it.

It sat there a few days like that, resting on my head like a worn-out welcome mat. When I finally broke down and washed it, the welcome mat slid off. Wrapping my head in a towel, I stepped out of the shower, trying to steel myself to look. Slowly I unwrapped the towel, and stared at my new self closely in the mirror. Every single hair was gone. Only one thing remained on my head—the last one of those stubborn, still crawling head lice.

Losing a breast I could handle; losing my hair was worse. This part of my new reality felt really *real.*

Bald. Need I say I never signed up for this? Maybe because my father had called it my crowning glory, my hair was the only part of my body I'd ever been satisfied with. Even in Miami humidity. Even with a bad haircut. Even on a bad hair day.

I couldn't accept who I was without it.

A scarf or hat covering a bald head was like publicly proclaiming I had cancer. I wanted to conceal my cancer—which called for camouflage or cover-up. Even a wig wasn't enough. I could spot one from a mile away. The wig needed a cover up of its own.

I never had been a hat person, but I was now, wearing one daily over the wig. Most of them came from a beautiful Brit who lived a few miles away in Carmel and was given my name by the oncologist we both saw in Los Angeles. Early on I was reluctant to see anyone or meet someone new, but Corinna insisted and showed up with an armful of hats that she had worn during her own chemo a few years earlier.

In addition to my new hat collection, I had a collection of wigs from my ongoing but futile quest to find one that looked *natural*. They looked the opposite of natural, sitting on white Styrofoam heads in my closet. This collection felt kind of creepy to me, but it didn't seem to bother Daniel, who loved to plop a wig on his head and parade around the house to make me laugh.

Unless I was asleep, one of the wigs was on my head. Even when I was asleep I wore a little cap. Because no one, and I mean NO ONE, was allowed to see me bald. Not the kids. Not V.

Not even ME. Alone in the bathroom with the door locked, I tried to avoid seeing myself in the mirror. My hair was such a big part of my identity and my wholeness that the sight of my bald head was too much to bear.

It was as if my real self had been lost along with my hair. What I saw in that bald person didn't fit any part of my identity. Stripped of what made me feel pretty and feminine, stripped of confidence, I saw weakness, fear, vulnerability. Qualities that were synonymous with unattractive and unappealing.

101

I had no clue that the opposite was true. Those qualities were me, too. Part of my authentic self. Parts of me I'd never seen before, certainly never examined up close. Being pared down to my essence was maybe the only way I could grow into that real self. Ironically, learning to see and live with my weaknesses ultimately became the key to discovering what I had also never fully tapped into before: my strengths.

Stand Up and Stand Out

Among the complications of my cancer was this ironic
scenario:

I was working for V's new business, focused on health and
wellness. Having cancer didn't make the boss's wife the perfect
poster girl for what we were preaching.

A big company event was scheduled at the home office, and a
lot of people would be coming into town. As I was undergoing
chemo, this event would mean interacting with a whole passel of
people who would know I had cancer.

I didn't want pity. And I certainly didn't want attention—
not when I was so self-conscious, missing my breast, all my hair,
my eyebrows, and eyelashes.

Skipping the event wouldn't be good for the business
strategically—and on some level, not good for me. Even so, six
weeks ahead of the event, sure there was no way I could pull off
looking confident and successful, I decided I wouldn't go.

Meanwhile I did travel hundreds of miles to Orange County
for a very different event: a gathering for women who were all
somewhere in our cancer journeys. Even with an extremely low
white blood cell count and little immune resistance, I was
desperate to be around people like me. Partly I wanted to get
accustomed to my new unwanted identity as a cancer patient.

The old me used to smile, laugh, love meeting new people.
The old me was full of life. This new me seemed solemn, scared,

small. I felt as if I carried around death like the new wig I wore. I had no idea how—or if—I would ever get the old me to come back.

None of the hundreds of women at this conference knew either the old me or the new me. I came alone and found a seat way in the the back of a crowded ballroom.

The woman on stage at the front of the room had had cancer too, and later she'd become a stand-up comic. Finishing her presentation, she asked if anyone in the audience would like to come onstage and tell a funny story about cancer.

Funny. Cancer. I found it ironic and impossible that she would put those two words in the same sentence.

She waited for a response. People looked around the room. No one volunteered.

Then I saw a hand go up. As if I was having an out of body experience, I saw it was my hand. I found myself rising out of my seat, walking through the audience to the front of the room and up onto the stage.

I was experienced and comfortable speaking in public. But comedy? This was some unknown part of me playing a new role.

I took the mic and looked out at the sea of women. In this room of total strangers I felt safe, more comfortable than I had felt since my diagnosis. So I relaxed and related my story. I won't do it here, since I tell this story in my TEDx talk, and much better than I could write it.

The incident I described had just happened a few days earlier, and involved me and my kids. From Mel Brooks I had learned the power of telling a story knowing that you can deliver the perfect punchline.

Bullseye. The burst of laughter swept onstage, filling me up and surrounding me with support. I understood the rush comedians must feel making a live audience laugh.

I also understood something else, something more personal and more important. I had harnessed a superpower. Science has proven that laughter improves the immune system, boosts energy, diminishes pain, and protects from stress.

The times we feel most powerless probably are the times we need it most. Nothing lifted me like the power to laugh in the face of what scared me most.

What washed over me was a feeling of release and relief. My sense of humor might be black, but it was back. With my newfound ability to wield humor as a weapon, I knew the real me would ultimately come back, too.

Something significant shifted by putting myself out there onstage honestly and bravely. I took this as a sign: maybe I had other powers hidden beneath the surface. I knew I could summon the strength to put myself out there again.

I had the perfect time and place: the upcoming company event. Instead of avoiding it, I chose to view it as an opportunity to flex my newly discovered inner muscles, to send a message to everyone—including myself. I would not just show up; I would put myself out there with guns blazing.

I wasn't going to feel my best but damned if I wouldn't look my best. In the next six weeks I couldn't grow back my boob, hair, and eyelashes. That I would have to fake. But a fashion statement could help me express my inner superhero.

What I wore outside could communicate my defiance and determination, and reflect the powerful me inside. My goal wasn't to remind people I had cancer; but to demonstrate that I could conquer it. The pink ribbon was brand new. I didn't consider wearing one. But color was the right idea and came to symbolize my spirit.

I looked through my closet in advance of the occasion. It was filled with appropriate clothes but none of them felt right. It was a business event; this was the 90's. I needed a power suit. And unlike all the black and neutral clothes in my closet, it had to be red.

The quest for a red suit became my obsession. Because the choices in Carmel were very limited, my friend Nancy met me after one of my chemo infusions in Los Angeles and took me for a shopping expedition focused on one goal. I tried on every single red suit in a twenty mile radius.

My final choice came from scouring one of the new shopping sites online. I was right. Red was my color.

I never wore the suit again. I didn't need to.

When I look at the picture today, what strikes me is that funny and cancer do belong in the same sentence after all. It's pretty funny that a woman with one breast from having cancer chose a double-breasted suit.

Where are the Casseroles?

Cancer left me so stunned that for the first time in my life, while trying to absorb the shock, I shut down socially. I withdrew. Back then, there was no social media. Friends and family were far away, and at first I shared my secret with very few people.

One of them was Shoosh, whose brother David was my college boyfriend. Shoosh and I grew closer when I moved to Carmel, though she lived three hours away so I didn't see her often. When I called her on a Sunday morning to tell her I had cancer, she could hear the bottom had dropped out of my world.

Though I've been there myself, I don't know the perfect words to console a friend in crisis. Does anyone? Do the words really matter? I don't remember what Shoosh said over the phone. I do remember that three hours later, she rang my doorbell. She must have jumped into her car the instant we hung up.

Until I saw Shoosh standing on my doorstep, I had no clue how starved I was for what she represented. Everyone is alone in Cancer World, but I felt alone in the real world, too. I had no mother; my father was estranged. Family and friends were far away at the time I needed them most. What did I need? I needed someone who cared about me, to see in my eyes how tortured I felt. I needed to see my own worries reflected in someone else's eyes. *I needed someone to show up.* I felt safer in those few hours I had with Shoosh, and I'll never forget her mission of mercy. It's one of those clichés—she was there when I needed her.

So was Judy. After my mastectomy in Los Angeles, Judy came home with me to Carmel. For the next week she did whatever I needed, from changing my bandages to fielding phone calls from people I didn't want to talk to, which was pretty much everyone except Judy. Because she was there. And because she understood.

We had met when she was first diagnosed twelve years earlier; and she was the only person I knew well who had breast cancer. I clung to the comfort of knowing another mother who had lived through the same nightmare. Not every friend can—or will—drop everything in her own life to come into yours when you need it. Judy did this not once, but multiple times. She would come to Carmel and stay with my kids when I needed to travel for treatment, giving them not only love, but hope—because Judy had survived, they believed Mommy would survive, too.

Having Shoosh and Judy show up early on made me extra conscious of what I was missing; for one thing, what I think of as crisis comfort food. A group of women circle the wagons around a woman in need, form a food chain, and magically, casseroles appear at her door every night. For years I'd seen and taken part in this ritual. So after my cancer diagnosis, I waited for the casseroles to start rolling in.

I never even got a tuna sandwich.

To be fair, I was living in a new community, working constantly. I hadn't had a chance to make friends yet. Plus it was summer vacation and very few people knew I had cancer. Which are all valid reasons to explain the lack of casseroles on our doorstep.

Only I didn't want reasons. I wanted casseroles.

Ultimately instead of asking, "Where are the casseroles?" I sent V for takeout.

I was still malnourished, a social creature starving for social contact. Over the previous year, I had occasionally shopped in a Carmel clothing store called Girl Boy Girl. The owner and her young employee took one look at me the day I walked in with my new size 2 body and new wig and immediately got it. Visiting the store more often was well worth the dip in my bank account because I so needed the lift in my mood. I used to joke that they were my cancer support group but what they provided was no joke.

Having no support system was not just a social issue but a health issue. With the focus on my physical health and what I was learning about cancer, I knew emotional health is an equally important part of the picture. A study had just been published at Stanford, proving that women in cancer support groups lived longer than those who weren't. Barbra was right: People need people.

My particular circumstances and timing topped off my mountain of stress. As I was starting chemo, my children were starting at two new schools, where I didn't know any parents at either place. Sensitive and self-conscious about meeting new people when I was bald, I was lonely enough to realize I had to be resilient. This was something new in my social repertoire: I would have to initiate everything myself. To adapt, I had to ask for what I wanted and needed.

As my first target, I chose a friend of V's named Carol who I had met once at a dinner. She worked at the school where Daniel was starting first grade. One morning during the first week, after I dropped off Daniel, I peeked into her office. I wasn't even sure she'd remember me. She did. At least she said she did.

So I plunged in with no preamble. "I don't know anyone at this school and I have breast cancer and I just started chemo and I'm really lonely. Will you be my friend?" I blurted out.

Carol got up from behind her desk and wrapped me in a big hug.

"Of course! Not only will I be your friend, but I'll introduce you to my friend Joanie, and she'll be your friend, too."

That afternoon when I came to pick up Daniel after school, Carol was standing by the carpool line, waiting to introduce me to Joanie, and they made plans for us to go out for coffee. What a difference it made to have friends who could give me a hug. Carol and Joanie were *there* for me.

That first connection made it easier to continue reaching out and ultimately to organically build relationships with amazing women in my new community. Taking those steps to get what I needed, I discovered others (who didn't even have cancer) wanted and needed the same things: camaraderie, closeness, someone willing to listen, and to laugh. Someone to *be there*.

I had taken friendships for granted. Cancer was no gift, but it taught me to value the gift of friendship as the treasure it is.

Trouble in Paradise

My treatment protocol involved two long, separate courses of chemo. Between them, my doctor gave me a "break": six weeks of daily radiation. That might qualify as a break in Cancer World, but I also needed a real one. For the kids' winter vacation, we planned a week in Hawaii. Having never been there, and growing up as native Californians, they refused to believe me when I promised them the ocean would actually be warm.

A beach vacation sounded dreamy, but as the trip got closer, reality started to penetrate my reveries. I had been going to the beach almost daily. But fall days at Carmel beach involve a wardrobe of sweat pants and jackets which wasn't going to cut it in Maui. And is there any woman who isn't self-conscious about her body in a bathing suit? Aside from Gisele, the rest of us have "issues," so imagine mine: being bald with one breast.

Mastectomy bathing suits with pockets inside to hold the fake boob looked too matronly. I bought a rubber prosthesis designed for swimming, tried on my one-piece suits, and chose one that would allow me to stash the fake boob safely inside. I was completely obsessed. Would people notice? Would I be able to swim with it? Would the fake boob fall out? Was the bathing suit too low-cut? Would anyone be able to see the scar across my chest? How about the other scar under my arm?

Then there was my hair. Or lack of it. I could feel a tiny bit of transparent fuzz coming in but I was still wearing wigs with hats over them. I planned to do the same thing in Hawaii no matter how hot it was.

As much as I love the ocean and looked forward to enjoying it with my children, my missing breast and hair could make swimming in it problematical. Today, a Facebook group of other survivors could solve all my problems, but back then, I used the best available resource. I sought the expert advice of my wig guru, Robin, who owned a hair salon and taught an American Cancer Society class called "Look Good Feel Better."

"No problem," Robin promised. "You can swim with the wig. Just take some eyelash glue and put a few drops on your head before you go in the water. That will hold the wig on and you'll be fine."

Eyelash glue and I were already acquainted, since chemo had left me without any eyelashes. So I added the eyelash glue to my arsenal and took off for Hawaii.

Eager to take the plunge into the ocean, I prepared beforehand in our room, dabbing on extra drops of glue to be sure the wig would remain securely fastened to my head. I tucked in the foam rubber breast and hoped it would stay where I put it. Then I headed out to the beach with the kids.

I couldn't help staring at the bodies of every other woman on the island—big, small, they all had what I wanted—two breasts and hair. I felt like a stalker, trying to keep my eyes off their cleavage and hungering for the normalcy of their lives.

The ocean was delicious, and I was deliriously happy to enjoy something fun with Alli and Daniel. I felt young and light and carefree and far away from Cancer World as I jumped the waves,

113

just the kind I liked, big and strong. Every few minutes I checked on the "foob" (what insiders call the fakes). It was still there. Giddy, laughing with the kids, I continued plunging into the surf, feeling exuberant and exhilarated…until I came up from a huge wave and saw both kids staring. Their faces told me even before I reached my hands up to my head.

The wig was gone.

In a pathetic but useless effort to cover my bald scalp, frantically I threw my arms over my head and started struggling to reach the shore. Daniel, eyes wide and completely speechless, backed away. Alli followed me up to the beach, trying to be helpful as she watched me grab my towel in a wild panic and wrap it around my head like a turban.

Everyone on the beach was staring. I would have appreciated the entertainment, too—if I was a tourist watching this tropical tragicomedy, rather than the main attraction. Alli hovered over me protectively, trying to shield me from my curious audience, while Daniel stayed in the water, trying to pretend he didn't know this lunatic on the beach.

In a burst of clarity I became both actor and audience. The insanity of the moment, plus the built up pressure of the past six months, exploded inside me. I became hysterical. Not crying. Laughing. Doubled up, choking, and shrieking. The accumulated emotions of cancer were simultaneously spilling out. All my careful planning and worrying about a breast slipping out of my bathing suit flew off along with the wig, stripping me of whatever dignity I imagined I had.

On top of my humiliation, I now had the comedic perspective to picture another scene that could take place in the near future. A young couple on their honeymoon, taking a romantic stroll at sunset along the shore, stumble over something washed up on the beach covered in sand. "What's this, honey?" she'd say sweetly, as he leaned over and picked up what looked like the hairy bedraggled remains of seashore roadkill: my wig.

I was bent over gasping for air, laughing like a maniac, when suddenly Alli leaped up and went running back into the ocean. "I see it, I see it!" Diving into the waves, she emerged triumphantly, holding up my wig like a runner with the Olympic torch. I'll never know how she managed to spot it from 200 yards away, one brown wig floating in the huge expanse of the Pacific Ocean. I got even more hysterical. Daniel remained as far away as possible to avoid any association with us.

When I finally calmed down, I rolled up the wig in a towel and took it back to the room, where I shampooed the ocean and sand out and hung it over the shower head.

I had a backup wig, which I wore to dinner. The next morning, the sand was gone, the wig was dry, and I plopped it back on my bald head. It never looked better. That day, I switched to swimming in the pool.

Musicals and Mojo

I sat on a folding chair in the All Saints school gym along with other parents and the student body, watching the annual musical. Daniel was seated on the floor in the front row with his first grade class, a prime spot to watch his 8th grade big brother and role model Robby onstage, playing Harold Hill, the lead role. Any performance by children is smile-worthy, *The Music Man* is especially wholesome and sweet, and *76 Trombones* isn't a tear-jerker. Still, I was sobbing. Robby didn't screw up or anything, I was crying because students couldn't participate in the musical until third grade, which was two years away for Daniel. I stifled my sobs as my brain silently begged: "Please let me live long enough to see Daniel in a musical. Just in the chorus."

Bargaining with the universe went on constantly. With the cancer cloud hanging overhead, little milestones of childhood went from sweet to sorrowful. In my mind, at bad moments, sometimes I was already dead and buried. Any soccer game, any parent-teacher conference could be my last. This made daily events not moments to be enjoyed in the present, but something already placed in my kids' past that represented pain in their future.

In addition to blaming myself that my children missed their father and friends in Los Angeles, now I blamed myself for expanding their suffering, making them feel different, exposing them to the harsh realities of life at tender ages.

116

People sent me books advising never to allow myself to think a negative thought. Are you kidding, people? Early on, practically every thought in my head was negative. Even more insidious was the idea that somehow getting cancer was my fault, not what someone facing it needs to hear.

Often cancer patients feel an expectation to live up to the image of the ballsy, brave, "bring it on" type. It makes you feel worse if everyone is telling you to be strong when all you feel is whiny and weak. Expecting yourself to face a crisis like a hero is just not realistic or possible for many people. Today there are so many support groups. What a difference it makes to have a safe place to vent, to bare your fears and your soul to others who have been there. I think we all deserve to feel sorry for ourselves sometimes, and to whine a little. Maybe even a lot.

Then we need to STOP whining. Because it is really important NOT to feel like a victim. The victim mode is hard to avoid with cancer, because you're instantly transformed into one, swallowed up by the medical system to be poked and prodded, helpless and out of control.

Getting out of victim mode can take some adaptation and attitude adjustment, whether it's cancer or something else. The good news is that we all have what we need to do this. We all have a source of inner strength that can bring out the best in people even at the worst of times. Somewhere inside each of us is the DNA of an ancestor who faced down a saber tooth tiger. The fittest survive, and that survival instinct has helped humankind adapt across the ages. It's so basic, it's there when we need it without having to think about it. But sometimes we need to consciously think about it in order to access it.

Ironically, my weakest point physically was when I began to tap into my emotional strength. My chemo was intense. A few days out of every chemo cycle, I didn't have the energy to get out of bed all day. I had adopted a strict diet regimen, eating no meat, no fat, no sugar, even existing without my beloved chocolate. For the first time in my life, nothing tasted good. I choked down four protein shakes a day, but my weight kept dropping. Add in the surgery to remove my ovaries, and I was the thinnest—and weakest—I had ever been.

My father-in-law stepped in at my low point to build me up. A life-long exercise expert, he explained that my lean muscle tissue was the source of my immune resistance and vitally important. He wanted me to start lifting weights.

Weights? I could barely lift my protein shake if it was in a heavy glass. But he insisted, so twice a week we met at the gym. He started me on a weights program that was so easy and light I didn't even feel as if I was working out, then he gradually increased the weights, repetitions, and the number of exercises. Just the act of working out, even with featherweights, made me feel more powerful, not just physically but psychologically.

I built on that feeling of power, just as anyone can do by finding people and things to motivate, inspire and support you. It's crucial to access and assert the psychological/emotional strength inside you, however you can.

Helping others is a proven way to keep your focus off yourself. It always works. I also kept a gratitude journal, which helped me appreciate and think about other things in my life besides cancer. The daily habit of feeling grateful transformed my thinking—soon I was able to experience those same sweet childhood moments with my kids as little treasures instead of little tortures.

Our minds are far more powerful than we typically give them credit for. When I changed our bad-luck wedding date, I truly believed it could and would change our lives. And it did.

You can find inspiration anywhere, in anything that speaks to you. If someone suggested I look for inspiration in the animal kingdom, I would have selected something graceful and sleek, like maybe a snow leopard or a swan. But one day my therapist made a random remark comparing me to a Clydesdale, one of those huge hefty horses pulling the wagon in the Budweiser commercials. I don't even drink beer, and at that time I was stick-thin, yet somehow that big bulky image resonated, and I adopted the Clydesdale as the identity of my stronger self. I even used it as my screensaver as a reminder to myself. Harnessing the power of my "spirit" animal was the perfect image to counteract my moments of weakness.

Typically I'm not Pollyanna-ish. I tend to skew toward the cynical. Cancer was a fertile source for comedy, as long as I could handle it black. It was healing and empowering to laugh at what scared me most. This concept of humor in cancer was completely counter-intuitive yet so powerful, I had to share it. So I found other cancer survivors with funny cancer stories and made a video called *What's So Funny About Cancer?* How could I possibly feel like a victim when I was laughing in cancer's face?

119

What helped me with my mojo won't necessarily work for someone else, but everyone can find his or her own way as long as they trust their gut instincts. Once you tap into that core strength, you are a survivor. That's something to honor, to celebrate, something you can call upon for the rest of your life. And you will. Because we're all survivors of something.

After the *Music Man*, I stopped sobbing at school musicals until *Joseph and the Amazing Technicolor Dreamcoat* six years later. That year Daniel moved beyond the chorus to play the lead role. This was more than I had bargained for and this time, the tears came from gratitude.

My Hero

Even during treatment, I was desperately seeking something, *anything* to give me an edge in the survival sweepstakes. A full year of chemo, surgery, and radiation wasn't enough to make me feel secure, especially when I projected ahead to when treatment would be over, often the worst time for those in Cancer World.

I was getting the best medical attention available. The conventional medical system had nothing more to offer. In the mid-1990's, alternative medicine was further on the fringes of the medical community and there were very few choices there, either. But I was open to anything. My basic strategy was to throw everything at cancer and hope something would stick.

In choosing what to try, mostly I stuck to my intuition—a gut feeling about programs or remedies that spoke to me. I definitely didn't fully investigate as I should have. I was willing to try something at least once if it didn't seem toxic or harmful. I tried herbs from China, nutritional supplements from Germany, a Japanese healer, tea from an Indian tribe in Canada, drops of a strange concoction from Israel. I regularly visited an alternative practitioner and took his recommended supplements—until the morning I got a call advising me not to come for my scheduled appointment that day because the FDA had raided the office early that morning and confiscated all the files.

None of these alternative choices were covered by insurance, and I want to stress how lucky I was that I could afford to try them. This included a personalized document from Ralph Moss, a leading figure in alternative medicine who would prepare private reports detailing options for an individual case. From the insane amount of reading I was doing, I was already well informed on many of the choices Moss presented. But his report included a few new ideas. One leaped off the page.

Dr. Georg Springer was a research scientist at Northwestern University in the 1970's when his wife was diagnosed with breast cancer and given less than a year to live. To help treat his wife, Springer drew on his background in immunology.

He had discovered certain antigens in cancer tissues that don't occur in healthy tissue. By developing a vaccine to produce antibodies against those antigens, he believed he could stimulate the patient's immune system to prevent a recurrence of breast cancer. Springer developed a unique treatment using antigens in the blood as a way to stimulate the body's own immune system. (Laurence Gonzales, in *MORE* Magazine)

Using his own treatment, Dr. Springer managed to extend his wife's life by several years. After her death he began giving his vaccine to other women with breast cancer to prevent recurrences. By the time I heard about him fifteen years later, he was conducting a long-term trial at Finch University of Health Sciences/The Chicago Medical School.

Springer described his discoveries, methods, and use of T/Tn antigens for early detection and prevention of breast cancer recurrence in studies he published in peer-reviewed journals. His sample was small, and his work was considered controversial because his program had no double blind study, no control group. For comparison, Springer matched his patients against data for recurrence and survival in age and stage matched controls.

Compared to survival statistics I was reading based on other available treatments, Springer's success was staggering. According to a 1995 report, of nineteen original patients, all survived for at least five years, and eleven survived for between ten and eighteen years. An independent analysis in 1999 showed a thirty percent increase in five year survival overall (all patients stage II-IV), and a seventy percent increase for patents with more advanced stage IV breast cancer.

He was even featured on the cover of *Life Magazine* in 1994.

Though his vaccine showed such promise, it was a long way from being available. Moss' report made this clear. Moss had recommended the Springer program to other clients like me, but no one had been admitted.

It can't hurt to try. Moss suggested this and I willed it to happen, convinced that somehow I could finagle myself in. Normally I was the opposite of aggressive, but having cancer mandated a new normal, my transformation from fearful to fierce.

I unleashed a flurry of letters and phone calls pleading my case, sending my medical records and everything Springer's staff requested. Nearly six months later, twenty-five years after I stood in my dorm room with the Yale admittance letter, I received a letter admitting me into the Springer program. This time, much more than I had at Yale, I truly felt I had won the lottery.

To stretch the analogy further, my orientation was a little like college, too. After my "graduation" from a year of cancer treatment, I spent five days in Chicago, mostly getting to know a few other women who like me, were newly admitted "freshman" just starting Springer's program. Sitting on folding chairs out in the hallway of his clinic, we shared stories. In our small group of women from all over the country, breast cancer was the single common thread. Springer accepted only patients whose cancer had spread beyond the breast. We were all stages II through IV.

On the first day, a nurse did a scratch test on our arms, which she checked over the next few days to gauge our skin reactions. I remember hearing that Springer had developed this test to detect the presence of cancer in its earliest stages, years before any other diagnostic tool that existed. One woman was there from Texas along with her twenty-something daughter, which brought to mind my twelve year old daughter home in California. By the time Alli reached her twenties, I hoped, thanks to Dr. Springer she might never have to worry about getting cancer at all.

My head was spinning with numbers again, no longer the survival odds from chemo protocols but the numbers from Springer's study. Those women had survived *ten years.* Ten years was an eternity. Enough time to see my children complete high school, enough time to get Daniel to the age I had been when I lost my mother.

I had so much faith in Dr. Springer's work that when I was finally ushered into a small examining room to get my vaccine, all I wanted to do was grasp onto his white coat and hug him. I didn't. He was a formal, polite man, though I could see warmth in his eyes. Profusely thanking him for allowing me into his program, I burst into tears.

The vaccine itself, combined with typhoid vaccine to boost the body's immune response, was delivered as two subcutaneous shots, spaced a few inches apart, to various sites on the body from the upper thigh to shoulders to lower back. The only side effects were flu-like symptoms, which most patients felt for a day or so following the injections. The day after getting the shots, we returned to the lab so our skin reaction could be measured by Springer's nurse.

Based on our measured reactions, we were assigned a date to be back in Chicago for the next vaccine. Each patient had a different schedule. At the beginning, this meant a trip from California to Chicago every six weeks. Later the visits were spaced out further. Some of the longtime patients, who had been getting the vaccine for more than ten years, only came a few times a year.

There was no end date. The paperwork we signed reiterated what Dr. Springer told us: his vaccine was intended to continue *ad infinitum*. We would be taking it for the rest of our lives.

As I made more trips to Chicago, I got to know some of the other patients; and I got to know more about the extraordinary life of the man who was saving mine.

Georg Springer was born in 1924 into a German family known for the enormous Springer-Verlag scientific publishing empire. Before devoting his life to breast cancer research, his distinguished career included appointments as Professor at the University of Pennsylvania, and Professor of Microbiology, Immunology and Surgery at Northwestern University.

Not only a brilliant scientist, Dr. Springer also was a humanitarian. He funded his own cancer research and built the Heather M. Bligh Research Lab, named for his late wife, at Chicago Medical School, part of Finch University in North Chicago. As much as I considered it a minor miracle that I ever discovered Dr. Springer, it was equally astounding that he gave his vaccine to me and to all of his patients during all the years of our treatment *for free.*

Even his sudden death in 1998 did not interrupt or end his dedication and devotion to his patients. Building on his already extraordinary legacy, Dr. Springer bequeathed the university funds to continue his research, his lab, and to continue administering his vaccine to his patients—still for free—for the rest of our lives.

In 1997 the U.S. Food and Drug Administration had approved Dr. Springer's vaccine as a Compassionate Use Investigational Drug, which meant it could be given to patients outside a standard clinical trial. Under these guidelines, my vaccine could be shipped to my doctor in California, who gave me the injections. I still flew to Chicago a few times a year for follow-ups.

The program continued but the future didn't feel as certain without Springer's leadership. The school fired some of his key personnel, including his designated successor; and sometimes I would hear stories that the school wanted to use Dr. Springer's funds for its own purposes.

I didn't believe the rumors until February, 2004, when a letter arrived from the school, newly named Rosalind Franklin University, notifying all the patients that the vaccine was determined to be ineffective, and was now discontinued. After more than twenty years, despite our continuing survival and despite Dr. Springer's wishes, his program was over. Just like that.

When I heard this news, first and foremost, I thought of myself. Almost ten years since my diagnosis, in theory I was out of danger. But I've seen too many recurrences, which is exactly what the Springer vaccine was intended to prevent. I believed it was doing that for me. I believed it was the reason I was alive.

I had tried and failed to help other women get accepted into Springer's program. When the school pulled the plug, I started thinking beyond myself. Millions of women could benefit from the application of Dr. Springer's work in the future. I owed my life to him, and I felt fate had presented me with a situation where I could make a difference. Ending the program, ending Dr. Springer's lifetime of work, simply felt unacceptable.

A few other women had been actively involved in keeping connections between the patients, but no one was preparing to challenge the closing of the program. I knew nothing would happen if I did not act.

As an advocate for my own health, I had grown to feel strong and capable. After picking up and rearranging all those broken pieces of my life, I had earned the power I felt down to my fingertips. It was now an integral part of my identity, part of my soul. I was a Clydesdale, strong enough to pull others along with me.

Had my father still been alive, he would not have recognized the person I had become. I still hated confrontation in any form, yet now I was about to pick a fight. A big one. Maybe I welcomed it on some deep level. My mission was so much bigger than me. Taking on a medical school didn't faze me in the least.

I found a prominent and wonderful Chicago attorney to take the case, and we brought a lawsuit against Rosalind Franklin University. After mediation failed, I got all fifty-two patients remaining in Springer's program to sign onto the case with me as the lead plaintiff. I had no idea that I was about to invest an enormous amount of work, time, and energy, that I was taking on a battle that would come to consume me nearly as much as my battle against the disease itself.

My goal was to use some of the remaining funds left by Dr. Springer for his research, and set up his vaccine program as a clinical trial at another institution. In this way, his pioneering work could be scientifically validated and developed for the benefit of generations to come.

Our legal team prevailed in the court battle and the patients settled with the school. From that point on, however, things didn't go as well. I wish I could say that we were able to get Dr. Springer's vaccine re-established and that it will be available in the future as an option to prevent recurrence. I'm legally bound not to disclose specifics of the case. In the end, it meant losing the battle that mattered most, not being able to seek a new home for the Springer program, and a huge disappointment for me.

In the course of writing this book, I was gratified to see Dr. Springer's published work cited in current studies by cancer researchers around the world.

His medical peers best express his legacy and scientific contributions:

Not only did Georg prove that these antigens can serve as effective diagnostic tools for the presence of human breast cancer, but he also pioneered the immunotherapy of breast cancer... Studies carried out with breast cancer patients, some of them for as long as twenty years after first diagnosis, indicated that Georg's immunotherapy had a significant suppressive effect on tumor growth...This approach is now widely accepted, but during most of his life and even at the time of his death, his major contributions to this field were not recognized by the scientific community at large.

Parimal R. Desai Ph.D.
Harry Schacter M.D. Ph.D.
Oxford University Press; *Journal of Glycobiology* 1999

Georg F. Springer, MD, spent over twenty years harnessing the potential of the immune system to combat cancer. Although his treatments were outside of the mainstream, he was anything but (coming from a very traditional medical and research background)...His work eventually led him to the development of what is known as "Springer's Vaccine" and his reported five and ten-year survival rates for stage II, III, and IV breast cancer with this novel T (Thomson-Friedenreich) and Tn antigen therapy are nothing short of amazing when compared against standard treatments.

Springer's work was truly ahead of its time. Perhaps someday it will be widely embraced and used, until that day we are left with a legacy giving us a new insight into immunity, cancer, and the elegant architecture of a breast cancer cell.

Dr. Peter D'Adamo, Creator of the Blood Type Diet, Author of NY Times Bestseller *Eat Right For Your Type*.

An Accidental Artist

Never in my life would I have used the word *artistic* to describe myself. I had almost no affinity for art. My childhood memories include playing sports, playing school, playing piano, but not playing with art supplies. Although my mom saved letters and report cards and stories I wrote, she never hung my art projects on the refrigerator or saved a scrap of my artwork. I always assumed she thought none of it was worth saving.

For ten years I attended camp all summer. Twice a week we had arts and crafts. I remember only one project I made, because I saved it for years. It was a mosaic made of small broken tiles on a wooden board, an abstract of three lines, each a different color, twined together like rope, surrounded by thick, bumpy white grout. If you saw this primitive mosaic, you would never suspect that its creator had any artistic talent whatsoever.

My college boyfriend was an artist, my closest friend from high school a highly respected art curator. I admired them. I aspired to understand what they did, what they could see in a work of art that I couldn't seem to see. I simply accepted it as fact: I was missing the gene for art.

I was shocked the first time someone used the word *artistic* in connection with me. In third grade, Daniel was asked to fill in the blanks on a form provided by his teacher for a Mother's Day gift. Choosing three words to describe me, he wrote "sentimental, outgoing, artistic." It's typical of Daniel that he had the intuition and insight to see so clearly at age 9 what I could not see at all.

Unlike his mother, Daniel actually had artistic ability. His kindergarten artwork was superior to anything I could have produced, so I thought he'd enjoy one of those little studios where you paint your own ceramics, which had just opened in Carmel. It also offered a way to reconnect with normal life as I was finishing up cancer treatment. So one afternoon I took Daniel to Glazes.

A little storefront faced out onto a pretty outdoor shopping area. Inside, shelves of bisque lined the walls—plates, bowls, mugs, boxes, figurines. Daniel chose a plate, I chose a small oval box, and we sat next to each other at one of the wooden tables in the center of the room. As usual I took notice of the people surrounding us, painting, laughing and talking. They were normal. They were happy. They didn't have cancer. They didn't worry that this could be one of the last happy memories their child would have of doing something fun with their mom. (They probably also weren't drama queens.)

Daniel finished his plate before I put on my first coat of paint. I couldn't expect a 7-year-old to sit around waiting for his artistically-challenged mother to finish her project, so a few days later, I went back to Glazes to finish my little box.

Very few people were in the studio on a weekday afternoon as I gathered up my supplies and sat alone at the same wooden table. Background music combined with a peaceful calm atmosphere relaxed me as I concentrated on painting the bottom of the box a pretty peach color with little blue-green squares. For the top, a peach rim around the edge with alternating squares. It took maybe an hour and a half.

A few days later I went back to pick up our masterpieces. Daniel's plate looked like it had been painted by a 7-year-old, and my box could have been done by a 9-year-old, if I can be generous to myself. The lines weren't straight, the paint wasn't even, the squares were wobbly, the design was uninspired.

Again it was mid-week and the shop was quiet. I had enjoyed painting, at least as much as it was possible for me to enjoy anything in those days, and I thought maybe I might try something else. V's birthday was coming up, so I chose a picture frame for this second project. After painting his birthdate, I was already out of design ideas, so I ended up with solid painted corners and a squiggly line along the edge.

If my first project looked like it was made by a 9-year-old, this one would have been credited to a 7-year-old. Even a husband who loves me would be hard pressed to appreciate it. No wonder Mom never displayed my artwork.

Although the end product was nothing to brag about, the *process* had been enjoyable. I wanted to go back and paint again. On some level I *needed* to go back and paint again. I had learned to trust my instincts, and my gut sent me back to Glazes.

By the fourth or fifth time, I was hooked. And I realized why. While I sat for those brief hours, concentrating on painting, I was thinking of nothing else. Which meant I wasn't thinking about cancer. That was the first time I realized it was even *possible* for me to stop thinking about cancer for any extended time.

Just to prove I don't exaggerate.

Though I was done with treatment, I wasn't done with fear. It tormented every waking and sleeping moment. I couldn't shake it.

One of the cruelties of cancer, or any crisis, is that it can become a paradox. You're fearful and stressed and everyone tells you the best thing is to escape from the fear and stress. Which is true...only you still have cancer, or what made you fearful and stressed in the first place. So when you find that you can't escape the stress and fear, you worry that you're making it worse— which makes you even more stressed and fearful than you already were.

There's no cure for cancer, and often there's no cure for this vicious cycle of stress and fear. I had tried meditation, music, yoga, walks on the beach. Nothing worked. Cancer was under my skin. I couldn't wash it off. It ate away at my soul. I had pretty much given up on finding anything to help me relax. Painting ceramics didn't look much like meditation but that's what it was.

At first I felt guilty about spending time and money on something that seemed frivolous. But I ignored the voice in my brain and listened to the truth in my gut. It was nourishing, it was healing, it was addictive, and it was good for me.

I kept going. I painted bowls. I painted mugs. I painted dishes. I painted sets of bowls. Sets of mugs. Sets of dishes. I painted personalized cookie jars for everyone I knew.

We have used this set of dishes in our home ever since I painted them.

Hand painted ceramics.

Sometimes I was there, impatiently waiting in my car even before Glazes opened, until finally the owner gave me a key. Inside, I had my own designated spot at the counter facing the front door. People came in and out, perused the shop, painted, and paid a foot away from where I sat, but I didn't see, hear, or notice anyone or anything else. I was in the zone.

Recently I read that this mental state has a name: *flow*. That makes sense. It was as if some trap door opened inside me and art flowed out. My brain turned off and I was using some other part of me. I wasn't thinking about what to paint. It just happened. It was as if my hands did all the work and I wasn't even connected to them. I would sit down every day with a few colors and just start. Colors, designs, ideas, appeared on the bisque almost like magic.

Creativity was released from my soul, from someplace deep inside me that I could not name, had not known existed. A friend once told me about an experience she had in early spring in upstate New York. Walking in an isolated area, she heard a deafening sound like a huge explosion. The violent noise turned out to be the break-up of an ice-bound river, water suddenly surging downstream, releasing all the pent-up energy of the river in a powerful and mesmerizing rush. Chunks of ice broke off, sweeping the river and parts of the land along with it. I've never seen a river burst from an ice-bound state, but imagining it is the closest I can come to describing my discovery of art.

The benefits expanded outside of Glazes, too. I was swept

For awhile, I was obsessed with painting teapots.
And there were many, many more.

into a world of color, shape, and design that I had never been able to see. Colors called to me. Patterns were everywhere—in nature, in clothing, even in my dreams. Sometimes I would wake up with a color picture in my mind of what I wanted to paint that day.

Every year I made a plate to commemorate the New Year.

Nothing changed regarding my talent and my ability to draw. I still could not draw a horse or a face if my life depended on it.

When I first married V, before cancer, we used to have family contests. Each person would start with a sheet of blank paper. One of the kids would choose a subject to draw—a dog, a tree, a house. We'd all get a few minutes, then we'd compare and vote on whose drawing was the best. The winner was always the same: V.

Years later, Alli spoke at an event, telling the audience the story of our little game, and how V was always the best artist in the family. Here's her take on how I had suddenly become artistic: "Chemotherapy apparently altered Mom's DNA."

At Glazes, I learned a few techniques from other people, but I would never copy or trace anything. And I didn't like to do the same thing twice. Creating something completely new, experimenting with colors and designs and patterns, was part of my process. Also part of my experience was how I felt there. I got cancer before I had connected to my new community. Karen Fenton, the owner of Glazes, was warm, welcoming, and wonderful. Glazes was where I began to attach, where I first felt at home in Carmel.

Finding Power in the Pieces

At first I wasn't interested when Karen introduced something new at Glazes: a form of mosaics called *Pique d'assiette,* designs made out of fragments of dishes and broken pieces of tile. Mosaics didn't resonate or register on my radar until Alli discovered them, which was a surprise in itself. Like her mother, she had shied away from art projects even as a toddler, so I was thrilled to see her interested in anything artistic. With no drawing required and a low barrier to entry, this was something we could share. While I painted at Glazes, Alli sat with me and made a few mosaic stepping stones for the backyard.

Once Alli opened my eyes to mosaics, mosaics opened my eyes to appreciate and experience art at a deeper level. They even altered the way I see the world. More than a passion or a creative pursuit, the myriad aspects of mosaics speak to my soul.

There's the element of connection. A mosaic is formed of inter-connected pieces that are meaningless in themselves, tangible proof that different elements connecting together can make a whole much greater than the sum of its parts. Mosaics also reflect the haphazardness of life, random shapes and colors jumbled together, mixtures with special appeal to my sensibility. I collected antique quilts, many of them crazy quilts created from fabric scraps. I can't sew, but was inspired to create my own art process, which I developed by putting painting and mosaics together.

I choose a combination of colors, and use that color palette to paint a group of tiles in different patterns that complement each other. After firing, I break the tiles into random pieces with a hammer, then arrange them into a mosaic, sometimes around a mirror. Since words have always been important to me, I like to paint words on tiles and insert them into my designs. Often I use as the focal point the words *You're Perfect*. The irony and the message express my art, which grew out of breakage and *imperfection*.

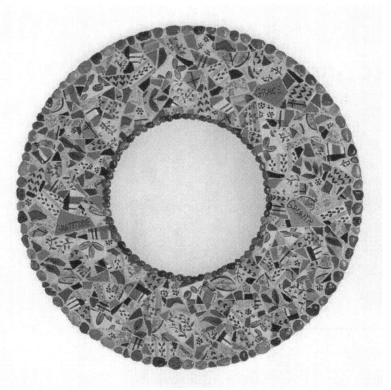

Growth. Grace. Gratitude. I painted every tile in every piece.

One of my favorites. I wish I had a better picture.

Even without words, making mosaics touched on a deeply rooted issue that I had just begun to explore: my need for perfection. The timing was no accident. For someone who found it difficult to accept imperfections in myself, a bald scarred body at first was harder to love. My art reflected my attitude as I grew into acceptance and authenticity.

Trying to counteract my perfectionist tendencies with a little Zen, I purposely left mistakes unfixed when I painted ceramics. A higher level of the same philosophy is called Kintsugi, a Japanese art form that uses gold to fill the cracks in broken pottery, making the breakage part of an object's history and value. Another life lesson found in art and a classic example of finding beauty in the *imperfections*. Whether you consider it art or therapy, mosaics couldn't be a more *perfect* match for a perfectionist: an art form made of pieces that are broken and imperfect to start with.

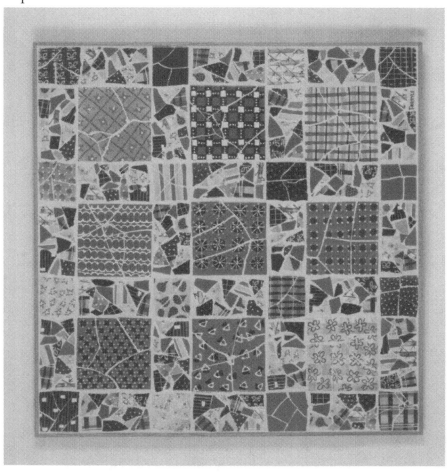

Inspired by quilts, like many of my pieces.

The more I made mosaics, the deeper my connection became. At the very deepest level, I think of mosaics as a metaphor for life itself.

Life can damage or break what is most beautiful and precious to us, as cancer had blown apart my world. Little by little, I realized I was picking up pieces of broken tile exactly as I was picking up the broken pieces of my life. I learned to see the beauty in the imperfections, as I created mosaic designs out of shattered fragments in all shapes and sizes. Rearranging broken pieces to make something unique, something different, something beautiful in a new way—my art process epitomized the process of resilience.

Opening my own studio was a huge step and transition. Instead of spending my days with creative material inside my head to *think* about, now I was immersed (and usually covered) in creative material I could *feel*, like paint and glue and grout.

Nothing was more healing or satisfying than working with my hands, creating art. Nothing else I had ever done could so reliably relax me, or nurture me. My hands could consistently put my mind into a mode that stopped negative thoughts and everything else from burrowing into my brain. In my studio I didn't even worry about my kids. A neurotic Jewish mother needed no other proof that this truly was magical.

Now I understood why my friend Christine spent most of her time knitting as she endured months of treatment for breast cancer. And why a successful entrepreneur I know does woodworking in his garage. I've seen it watching friends garden, and when I've conducted mosaic workshops for cancer patients at the American Cancer Society's Hope Lodge in New York. Scientific studies prove that it's more than a release, more than relaxation. Working with your hands is therapy.

The body is a miracle, capable of healing itself in many ways. There's so much we don't know or understand. We've only scratched the surface of human capability, barely begun to honor or harness the power of the mind/body/spirit connection. In addition to what we already know about healing by using our heads—and our hearts—I think we also hold the power in our hands.

The Breasts that Shook the World

My breasts made an impact on my life way out of proportion to their size, their function, or their value. They were prominent at the very beginning, as if they were trumpeting their importance right from the start.

Growing up on Miami Beach, I spent most of my time by the pool or ocean, and I'm topless in almost all the pictures of my early childhood. I couldn't even walk yet, and I already had definite little mounds on my chest.

I can't remember a time when I wasn't self-conscious about them. No wonder I avoided bathing suits.

Just to prove (again) that I don't exaggerate. I had breasts from birth.

Next to me in every picture, only 18 months younger, there was my sister Carla, with her skinny little boy body. Carla topped out in adulthood at barely 5 feet and 95 pounds. My breasts at age 2 were the size my sister's breasts are now.

146

By fourth grade, I was taller than my mother. And I already had larger breasts. Having cleavage is cool but not when you're 9.

Remember, I'm only 18 months older than Carla. Here I was 10 or 11; I can practically feel my pain. The bathing cap is the capper.

I have no idea when I actually started needing a bra. I do remember my mom pressuring me to get one. I refused. No one else wore a bra, and I didn't want to be different. Mom didn't ramp up the pressure until she felt it was absolutely necessary. Finally she marched me off to get a bra when I was in 4th grade.

I remember taking Alli to Victoria's Secret for her first bra—a flimsy, stretchy, soft little scrap that she had fun choosing and trying on. For me, the first bra fitting was serious business, supervised by a very serious saleslady who looked like a prison matron and who joined my mother and me in the dressing room for this female rite of passage. Clearly in charge, she inspected me up and down, measured my chest, and stood with a dead serious expression, arms folded, watching me try on one bra after another.

It had to fit perfectly. No daylight would pass between my breasts and the material that covered them, and the bra lady taught me how to achieve that. You bent over and jiggled each breast around inside the cup until it snapped into place. This experience was so deeply embedded that I continued to do this motion every time I bought a new bra for the rest of my life, as if the bra Nazi was still watching.

She also chose the bras. The lingerie equivalent of orthopedic shoes, they were stiff, structured, white cotton fastened at the back with a row of hooks. The cups came to a point, like Madonna's famous cone brassieres decades later.

My first bra was a size some women would be satisfied to reach in adulthood. But wearing a 34B in 4th grade was not a status symbol. It was a torment. My self-consciousness rose to new proportions. Besides feeling embarrassed about my precocious development, I had an additional worry—that little piece of telltale elastic across my back was a target for all the boys in my class who tried to snap it.

Since my boobs were a source of annoyance and embarrassment, it was many years before I had the faintest idea that any other girl might be envious. Why would they be? What was the big deal about having big ones? For one thing, I liked sports and they flopped all over the place. Since sports bras were not yet on the drawing board, my breasts were in the way, an irritation, another part of me that was TOO BIG.

Even when I grew up I didn't show them off; and I didn't appreciate or enjoy the attention they attracted. Though this sounds far more weird than it was, there was a time when the male most interested in my breasts was my dad.

Having little insight into feminine mysteries, Dad inherited the job of steering me through issues of emerging adulthood. He was in way over his head. I might have shared experiences of sexuality with my mom, but my dad? By unspoken mutual consent, Dad and I followed a policy of "Don't Ask, Don't Tell."

During college, I strategically mentioned to him that I was having irregular periods, and Dad played right into my hands, connecting me with his doctor friend in New York who wrote me prescriptions for birth control pills over the phone without ever seeing me. I doubt my father ever suspected that his friend was providing me with a free pass to the sexual revolution. But Dad definitely took notice when I came home from college.

My breasts were positioned at the intersection of two tumultuous social changes, sexual freedom and feminism. Thanks to the pill, my boobs were larger than they had ever been. Thanks to feminism, I didn't burn my bras but I stopped wearing them. My mammoth-size mammaries swung freely under t-shirts and peasant blouses. That prompted Dad, feeling it was his duty, to venture into territory that would have been my mother's.

He didn't worry that my breasts would define me or attract the wrong kind of attention. His worries were more concrete. Without the support of a proper "brassiere" at 20, he warned me that someday when I was older, I would have "pendulous, sagging breasts."

I heard that phrase repeated every time he saw me. And he was absolutely right. My breasts would sag. If I still had them.

My boobs leaped to the top of my priority list once again when I made the leap from birth control to birth. Breastfeeding was a given, vital to giving my children the right start in life. My breasts came to represent my ability to be a good mother. Before giving birth to my first child, I painted beautiful mental pictures like you'd see in diaper commercials, serene scenes in soft focus of a contented mother nursing her contented baby.

Reality was in sharp focus, and looked a little different. One hour after arriving home from the hospital with Alli, I was bent over the kitchen table, dangling both boobs into a bowl of ice water. My tits had turned into torpedoes pointing straight out from my chest. They were the same size, same shape, and as hard as fully inflated footballs. They were also hot to touch, and engorged to such an extreme that no milk would come out.

My brand new baby and I were both sobbing. Alli from hunger, since milk doesn't easily come out of footballs. My tears were from frustration and failure to play my proper role in the idyllic mother scene. Here I was, a college graduate, yet I could not manage to do what illiterate, prehistoric women had done since the beginning of time.

Within twenty-four hours I had mastitis, a full blown infection of the breast, which felt like the flu. Though antibiotics helped the infection, breastfeeding wasn't happening right, and I had no idea why. But hey, this wasn't brain surgery. Determined to succeed, I sat on the couch hour after hour while my baby used me as a human pacifier. I soon had the sorriest looking nipples on the planet. And pain to match.

Who knew you could butcher such basic stuff? In those days there weren't many resources available but I tracked down breast consultants for personal lessons. My boobs were handled by the best in the business, who helped me position my child with pillows and shoved her head onto my breast to help her latch on.

Despite the experts, little improved. I continued to hang on, and so did Alli. The La Leche League asked for permission to photograph my nipples as an example of cracked nipple syndrome. They told me reverently that I had the worst case they had ever seen.

My doctor and my husband both begged me to give up and bottle feed. I refused to stop, standing firm on my ability to withstand pain, and gritting my teeth every time I opened the flap of that nursing bra.

Weeks later, another expert eventually explained that it wasn't about me. It wasn't about latching on, or positioning, or pillows. Alli wasn't sucking properly, due to some immaturity she would soon outgrow.

So much for Mother Nature. I waited it out. And I finally got to live that idyllic image of motherhood, nursing Alli almost a year, and then Daniel, who managed to do it correctly from day one.

After feeding my children, my boobs lacked their previous bounce, but they had done their job. I tucked them away mentally and physically without giving them another thought for the next few years.

Until suddenly, there they were on center stage again. With no warning whatsoever, my breasts betrayed me, turning on me overnight. Accused of conspiring to commit treason, my right breast was tried by a jury of doctors, and found guilty of premeditated murder. As the intended victim, I also served as the judge. I sentenced my breast to death.

"Should I have the other breast taken off, too?" I asked Dr. Guiliano before my mastectomy.

"The other breast shows no signs of cancer. There's no reason to take it off," he replied.

Do it. You won't have to worry about cancer on the other side. Why keep one breast? I ignored the voice in my head.

"What about reconstruction? Should I have it now?" I asked.

"With just a mastectomy you'll recover more quickly and you can start chemotherapy sooner."

As translated in my head: *Your cancer is growing like crazy so we can't waste time with reconstruction. And why bother with more surgery? You're going to die soon anyway.*

I didn't push the point. Cosmetic issues were a low priority. With potential death at the top of the list, everything else drops way down.

Very soon I already wished I had trusted my instinct and taken off the other breast. Among the many complications of my pathology report, among the several types of cancer present in my breast, I had multi-focal cancer. This is less common, but far more likely to spread to the other breast. So having my other breast off was not paranoia but a medical recommendation.

I was reasonably sure I would die before I had to deal with reconstruction, anyway. Here's a real indication of my mental state: I figured if I lived long enough, having that other breast off would be something to look forward to.

A year after my diagnosis, I was ready: a mastectomy for my left healthy breast, and reconstruction on both sides. The tram flap was just becoming fashionable. This was a brilliant innovation, using excess abdominal tissue to create breasts, making this one of the very few perks for women who need mastectomies. New breasts and a tummy tuck at the same time: one stop shopping. For me, it was also my chance to fulfill a lifetime fantasy—having a size A cup.

Another fantasy was to be very thin, and I was, thanks to cancer, chemo, a low fat diet and stress. Only according to the plastic surgeons I consulted, being so thin meant no tram flap surgery. I didn't have enough tummy tissue to make even one A size breast, let alone two.

You know how they say, "be careful what you wish for?" This was a perfect example. You know how they also say, "So much of life is timing?" Another example. Had I waited a few years, I could have had any size breasts I wanted. Today I have enough tummy tissue to make boobs for the whole neighborhood. Back then, my only option was implants.

As described to me by the plastic surgeon, this was a simple surgery with an easy recovery. I'd remove the remaining breast and get implants inserted on both sides. The first phase of implants—called expanders—were like collapsed balloons. In the beginning my chest would still be flat. In a few weeks, I would start having the implants inflated little by little until I was the size I wanted to be. Seemed simple enough. On to LA for reconstruction.

I woke up after surgery, expecting to feel better than I had after the first mastectomy. But something was terribly wrong. I felt like an elephant was sitting on my chest. I could not take in a breath because of the enormous pressure.

When I asked my plastic surgeon, I got the feeling this wasn't the first time he had patients complain about this elephant. I later asked an acquaintance who had the same surgery if she'd had this pain. Yes, she remembered the elephant, she admitted. "I didn't tell you beforehand because I didn't want to discourage you from having reconstruction."

It took a while to adjust to the pain but I hung in there, anticipating the day when I could go braless in t-shirts and look like a boyish yet sexy model. As soon as I could breathe without gasping, I made plans to go to LA to have the expanders inflated.

Before my trip, my left breast suddenly turned bright pink. (To be completely accurate, I had no breast. The area where my left breast used to be turned pink). I called my LA doctors, who assumed I had an infection and put me on antibiotics. When that didn't help, I went to a local plastic surgeon. The nurse who entered the examining room gave me a gown and smiled. I had never been in this office, but she seemed to know me. She told me she was Charlie's mom.

Charlie and Daniel had been in the same class for a year and a half and were close friends. I surely had met his mom at school functions, and Daniel had been to her home. Me—the ultimate hands-on mom who used to drive on every field trip and attend every possible classroom activity—had no idea who this woman was. That gave me an inkling of how far I was removed from normal life.

Meanwhile Charlie's mom could not help with my bright pink breast, nor could the plastic surgeon nor my medical team when I got down to LA. I needed yet another surgery to remove the expanders I'd just spent months suffering from. In the end, it turned out there was no internal infection, nothing wrong with the expanders at all. My body simply rejected them.

My breasts were still occupying the spotlight even when they weren't there.

So I wasn't going to get those small perky breasts. I always envied girls who were flat chested, and now I was one of them. Only after two mastectomies, being flat is far different.

Flat-chested women might have breasts the size of raisins, but they have breast tissue and muscle under the pectoral area. They have nipples. They look flat, but natural. I have no nipples, no tissue, and no muscle where my breasts used to be. My chest is concave in some places, lumpy and bumpy in others where the bones of my ribcage stick out.

Luckily I never strongly identified with my breasts. Although they'd always been attached to me, I wasn't really that attached to them. They helped my clothes look and fit better, but that could be camouflaged. They nourished my children, but that functionality was finished. At times they played a starring role in my sex life, but V continued loving me no matter how many body parts I lost. So what was the big deal about not having breasts?

If I sound flippant, well, I wasn't really. But when you weigh breasts vs. life? Not much of a contest. I had no boobs, not even silicone or sagging ones, but I was *alive.*

This was not a catastrophe, just another broken piece. I could adapt. Getting dressed every day, the routines were now a little different. Panties, bra, breast, breast, then the other stuff. Buy bras that were not too low cut, so the fakes don't pop out. Tuck little rubber mounds into my bras and hope they stayed where I put them. Eliminate from my wardrobe tops that were low cut, clingy, or strapless. Very sheer clothing needed a protective layer. Mostly having no boobs was inconvenient.

On the other hand, there were plusses. I could buy breasts in any size I wanted. No erect nipples in cold weather or air conditioning. No bouncing during exercise if I left my boobs at home.

But wearing fakes had their own set of issues. I still wore normal bras, and sometimes those "foobs" had a mind of their own. After an hour of practice swings with an instructor at a golf range, I looked down to see what Alli called the "uniboob." Both of my rubber breasts piled on top of each other right in the center of my chest. The instructor, an unflappable Brit, surely noticed, but never said a word.

Getting dressed for a business meeting in a Chicago hotel, I noticed a crack in one of my foobs, oozing out gummy stuff that looked like a melted marshmallow. Not even trying to explain the nature of my emergency, I called Housekeeping with an urgent request for tape. I figured a little scotch tape could hold the foob together till I got back to California. What I got delivered to my room, and used, was thick packing tape, so strong I could have sent that foob UPS to Africa.

Twice both of my fakes floated out of my bathing suit while I was snorkeling. I managed to recover them while surrounded by giant turtles in Maui. But the second time, at the Great Barrier Reef, I was so mesmerized by the scene underwater that until I climbed out of the water, I didn't even notice they were gone. I always wondered if some tourist thought they'd discovered a new species of coral down there.

Sometimes I forgot to wear them. In our small town, people who saw me in the morning at the gym *without* boobs could run into me a few hours later *with* boobs. I used to wonder what they would think.

We all wonder what people will think. Truthfully though, the person who thought most about how my body looked had always been *me*.

It was weeks after my first mastectomy before I finally worked up the courage to look in the mirror at my body without my right breast.

Next to my left breast, a scar ran almost six inches from the center of my chest to my armpit. My right side was lumps and bumps and bones and skin.

About to step on the scale, I wondered what would I weigh if I still had the breast. How much did one C-cup weigh? One pound? Two?

I was having chemo and I was thinner than I had ever been. Instead of making me happy, it was the opposite. Every day I weighed less and I worried. How long could this go on?

My body was ravaged. I was scrawny. I was bald.

One day I looked in the mirror and made a silent solemn promise to myself.

If I survive I will never again complain about a bad hair day or being too fat. I will love my body no matter what it looks like.

I've kept that promise for twenty years.

Sure, I wish I had breasts—not to mention a waist. But my body met the challenge of cancer, giving me the precious gift of life. And I have never loved my body more than I do today.

Over the years I've grown into what sounds like a cliché: *authenticity*. Partly this comes with age, which makes it easier to let go of body image issues we spend our lives struggling over. To use a word I don't ordinarily use, it's *empowering* to discover at some point that you don't give a shit what other people think. It's equally empowering—and authentic—to embrace what we think ourselves.

Among the many truths I discovered is that I felt very satisfied with my very imperfect body. It didn't take rocket science to figure out that fake breasts did not go with my authentic self. I was totally ready to let them go.

I could adapt to flatness as I adapted to everything else. To match my adjusted mindset, I adjusted my wardrobe to include scarves, shawl collars, looser styles, and I was good to go.

Going breastless permanently and publicly would have been unthinkable when I was so self-conscious a few years earlier. When I first met a few survivors bold enough to go flat from day one, I was astounded at their courage. Now I'm one of them. Today more women are choosing authenticity after breast cancer, privately and publicly expressing their altered realities in their own unique ways.

As I have. Some friends didn't even realize I had breast cancer until they read my first piece for the *Huffington Post*, about how and why I stopped wearing fakes. For me that was a step forward and a statement, the same statement I started making through art.

Thinking Outside the Bra

People had been urging me for years, "Use your cancer in your art." For me, "cancer" and "art" didn't belong in the same realm or even the same sentence. Cancer represented what was most dark and depressing in my life; art represented what was happy and colorful.

Inspiration struck from an unexpected source while I was at Glazes, painting a piggy bank for a personalized baby gift. I doubt I could recreate the chain of thought that led to my epiphany. But at some point, with its little round tail in the middle, the butt of that pig started looking exactly like a breast, ripe and round with a nipple in the center.

Eureka! Oink! I sacrificed another piggy to the cause, cut the bank in half and painted the butt in flesh tones. Using that breast/butt as the focal point, I surrounded it with broken tiles in the shape of a woman's torso and there it was: my first cancer-inspired creation.

If a pig's butt could be a breast, what else could be a breast? From there it was just thinking out of the box. Or the bra. Master locks. Wine corks. Golf balls. That was the birth of Boobalas, a whimsical collection of mosaics shaped like women's torsos with breasts as the focal points.

Once again, art opened my eyes to see the world in a new way. Everywhere I looked, I saw something that could stand in for boobs. Hot and cold faucets. Ceramic pears. Door knockers. Who could get away with poking fun at our society's obsession with breasts better than a woman who doesn't have any at all? Boobalas add another benefit of my art in addition to stress reduction: a way to work out lifelong issues surrounding my breasts using humor and attitude. It's far more creative and cheaper than therapy.

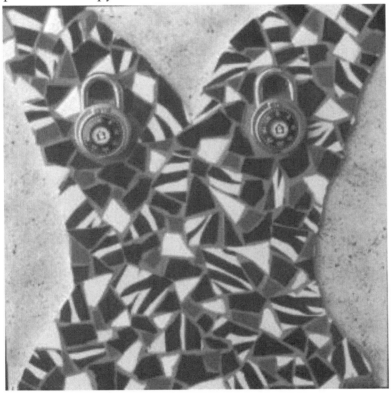

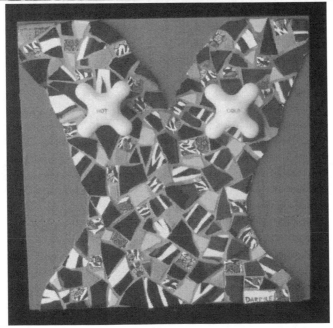

163

Although the message wasn't just for fun. Some Boobalas represent women after breast cancer. With two breasts, one or none, we all have something in common. Cancer has come along and blown apart our lives. We pick up the broken pieces and assemble them into something different from how we were before. After cancer, all in our own shapes and sizes, uniquely authentic and imperfect, we're still feminine and still beautiful, with our broken pieces put together.

I hope Boobalas offer perspective to all women—and to men—about where breasts fit in the big picture. They may be an appealing part of our bodies, but they don't determine a woman's beauty or femininity, and they don't define who we are.

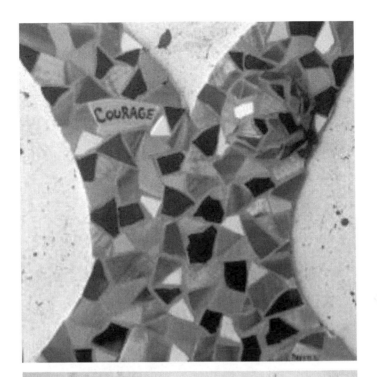

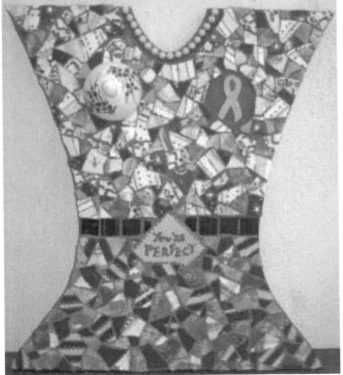

Why Me?

When I had cancer, I remember asking this question a lot. Unlike Moses or Joan of Arc, I never got an answer. At least not from a higher power. The best answer I heard was, "Why *not* me?" Maybe it's because I'm Jewish, and Jews like to answer a question with another question.

For months this plagued me. Why did I have to suffer? Why was life unfair? Why didn't bad things happen to a bad person instead? I could easily have filled in some names.

I'm not a philosopher, and I'm not terribly introspective, so I wasn't asking this question on a profound level. Nothing existential that could have puzzled someone like Spinoza or Maimonides—maybe not even Dr. Phil. Pretty quickly I stopped asking a thousand times a day and dialed it down to a hundred times a day. Ultimately I got through a day without asking more than a few times. And then at some point, I stopped asking at all.

I never got an answer but I stopped asking because the question didn't apply anymore. I was alive. Besides, other people had the same question. People who were also good. People who had cancer, and people who had other things, often far worse.

Then a funny thing happened. Further down the road, after I stopped asking and even stopped thinking about this very much, I started asking again. "Why me?" Only now I was asking the question in reverse: not, why was I going to die, but why had I lived? Why had I lived when my prognosis was so dire and my odds so poor? Why had I lived when others were dying?

Often called survivor's guilt, it's also felt by people who walk away from plane crashes or collapsed buildings. How can you not feel guilty and confused? Why were you chosen to live? Is there a mission or purpose meant for me? Is there something I'm destined to contribute, some reason I was allowed to live?

"Why me?" remains a question without an answer. And I think that's how it should be. If I knew the answer, maybe I would stop searching.

Dear Mom:

You've been gone longer than you were here. And I still feel cheated.

Over the years I gradually began to grasp what I was missing. Without you there, every accomplishment, holiday, and joyous event was bittersweet. You never got to plan a wedding, share a pregnancy, hold a grandchild. In every crisis of my life, I've longed for your counsel and your comfort.

I miss you not only for the big things, but the little ones, the simple things many people take for granted.

I imagine how we'd spend a few hours on an average day. Linking arms as we walk. The sound of your voice. The strand of pearls you always wore. Joy—the word for your scent and your substance. Your personality that was both calm and vibrant at the same time. Your smile, your biggest smiles just for me, pride and love visible in your eyes. No one else looked at me like that. No one ever will.

It wouldn't matter where we would go. Maybe the beach. You were always convinced the ocean had healing powers. Maybe shopping. No one had better taste, or a better eye for a bargain.

Maybe out to lunch. We would share not just the food. We'd share laughs. We have the same one, hopelessly hysterical, soundless and breathless with tears pouring down our cheeks.

We'd share intimacies and news. Who else would want to hear endless stories about my kids?

No day would be complete without sharing the most important stuff. I inherited the chocolate addiction, and as you always said, there's nothing in life that can't be cured by an ice cream soda. So maybe we'll share one. (Who am I kidding? We'll each have our own.)

Mom, being with you would be perfect. A perfect fantasy.

Because there are no lunches. No laughs. No chocolate.

None of those little things. And none of the big things, either.

There's nothing at all.

I miss you whenever I see mothers and daughters together. Any time. Anywhere. Even on Facebook.

Losing you meant losing my touchstone. Maybe the only times I ever felt perfect were when I saw my reflection—and unconditional love—in your eyes.

Your legacy and greatest gift is that you were the mother I aspire to be.

I haven't forgotten about you, but I have forgotten. I've forgotten how you walked, how you talked, how you laughed. My memories are dim and faded and vague. Many are erased. I've tried to keep you alive for me and my kids. But it's impossible to breathe life into a photograph. You're only alive to me in my dreams.

In real life, you never met either of my husbands.

You never knew my children.

You never really knew me.

And worst of all—I never really knew you.

On My Mother's Birthday

On my mother's birthday every year, long after her death, I remember feeling resentful. It still seemed unfair that my mother had to die while other mothers got to live. On that day I resented every mother on the planet, but there was one person who got the largest share of my bitterness: my mother's sister.

She and her family lived in New York, and even when my mother was alive we rarely saw them. After Mom died, the most obvious person to step in never did. Never visited, never called, never wrote.

She was my mother's only sibling, my link to my mother's past. That they were completely different in every way only made it worse. How could the universe take away someone who stood for everything good and leave alive someone who was, in my mind, not half the human being my mother was?

The years passed, bringing more physical and emotional distance. I stayed in touch sporadically with my cousin, my aunt's daughter. In almost forty-five years, I saw my aunt three times: once at a funeral, once at a wedding, and the day after the wedding. My sister and brother, who didn't go to the funeral or the wedding, never saw her or heard from her at all.

Life went on. Memories and hurts dimmed until my mother's side of the family was no longer a raw gash but a scar. Then one day out of the blue a few years ago, the phone rang. When I answered, someone said my name. Just one word, I knew instantly who it was, and the prickles rose on my neck as soon as I recognized my aunt's voice.

She wanted to tell me about some of her life's challenges, and how her personal problems had prevented her from reaching out to us, her sister's children. And she needed something else. Because she was in pain. I could hear it.

"Can you forgive me?" She was in tears. "For not being there for you?"

Forty years after my mother had died, I could only imagine what demons had prompted her sister, and what it took to make that call. I had lived all those years feeling distance and resentment and I didn't hesitate for one instant to tell her how I felt.

"Of course I forgive you," I told my aunt. And I did.

Motherless Daughter

The note came with a small box when I married Howard, and it was the only wedding gift that made me cry.

Dear Darryle,

When I was a bride, my mother gave me a collection of her best recipes. I still love seeing her handwriting on them as I look something up in my recipe file.

*So for your wedding present, I have copied for you **my** best recipes. You may never get to cook them yourself but I'd like you to have them. They are associated with happy days, happy evenings, and I send them to you with all my love.*

It wasn't from my new mother-in-law; Howard's mom died years before we met. This note came from the woman I once thought might be my mother-in-law, the mother of my college boyfriend, David.

There were no handwritten recipes handed down from my own family, since I come from a long line of Jewish mothers on both sides who couldn't cook. David's mom was right. I never did make many of her recipes. But I treasure her wedding gift to this day, as a window into something I never had and always wanted: a lifetime mother/daughter bond.

Although I felt deprived, I didn't draw close, seek out, or reach out to anyone who could have played the role of surrogate mother in my life. I wish I had. I also didn't realize how deep the loss cut. I assumed grief was a torrent of pain spilling out soon after a loss. I had no idea that grief could work in reverse, plugging up emotions for years to come.

In my forties I read Hope Edelman's newly published book *Motherless Daughters,* and a few years later, *Motherless Mothers.* I felt like a lost soul wandering in the desert who stumbles across an oasis, and frantically scoops up water with her bare hands. This was my first glimpse into the souls of others walking around with similar holes in their hearts, and it's when I started to appreciate how deep that hole could be. Reading about lifelong ramifications of losing a mother early in life, I felt less alone, more comforted, more forgiving of myself for fears, anxieties, and insecurities I had never understood.

I wasn't sure I wanted to become a mother at all; but it was when I became a mother that I finally put together the broken pieces my mother left behind. Instead of *finding* the mother I had lost, I *became* the mother I had lost. It was as if I had spent my life searching for something that had been inside me all along. Having children was the nourishment I had been starving for and nothing else has, or ever will, satisfy me the same way.

Consciously or not, motherhood also provided the path by which I could extend my mother's life, validate and value her legacy. I aspired to be the kind of mother I had had, and my identity as a mom superseded everything else. My heart seemed to overflow with maternal feelings whether directed toward my own children or someone else's child. And I began to appreciate the significance of those other moms, women who are not our mothers but who can play pivotal roles in our lives.

Towards the end of her life, my mother had asked Aunt Helen to watch over her children. Aunt Helen promised Mom that she would, and stayed as close as she could, long distance. Once I was a mother myself, I finally opened my eyes and my heart, and let her in.

Alli was two and we were hoping for a second child. Before getting pregnant again, I needed surgery to remove a benign fibroid tumor which would require several nights in the hospital. How was that going to happen when I could barely rip myself away from Alli during the day? Even having Howard at home wasn't enough to calm my anxiety about leaving her overnight, which I had never done once since she was born.

Desperate mothers call for desperate measures. I called Aunt Helen. I hadn't seen her in years; she had never met Alli or been to Los Angeles. Her fear of flying might have rivaled my fear of separation from Alli. But she got on a plane and came from Miami, bringing me baked goodies and peace of mind.

The impact of her presence was profound. During the times that Howard needed to be with me at the hospital, Aunt Helen stayed at home with Alli. This was the first time Alli had a babysitter who wasn't paid to watch her. Someone who loved her.

A classic Jewish mother, Aunt Helen worried that she would overwhelm Alli with too many kisses and exuberant hugs. Has any kid ever suffered from too much love?

For me this experience was even more meaningful. Having Aunt Helen in my home helped me heal from a twenty year loss; and find peace with pieces my mother left behind. I was over the moon, feeling so safe, so secure, so different than I had felt since having children. When I gave birth to Daniel, Aunt Helen came out again and stayed a month. If I had my way, she would have relocated to California permanently.

Her occasional visits and ongoing long distance relationships with my children gave them an inkling of what it might have been like if my mother had lived. My kids called her Aunt Helen, too, but she was the closest they will ever come to knowing how it might have felt if they had a grandmother. And what Aunt Helen provided me was a unique perspective that could not be duplicated. When I turned 60, she jokingly reminded me that she had changed my diapers. Having her love was a precious gift for which I didn't and couldn't have ever thanked her enough.

With families that are fragmented, scattered, and blended, we aren't all lucky enough to have relatives who are there for us geographically, physically, or emotionally. If we're really lucky, we have friends who define what family truly means, even though our mothers told us blood is thicker than water. It's a testament to the person she was that my mother inspired a

Aunt Helen was about 92 when this was taken, still sharp as a tack.

175

friendship which endured so far beyond her lifetime. Aunt Helen kept her promise to my mother till the day she died at 96.

The Patriarch

In every family there comes a time when relationships reverse and there's a changing of the guard. It's the shifting of generations, part of the circle of life. Typically this change moves at a glacial pace, but sometimes it can happen in an instant.

That's what happened in our family. The kids were very young and I was still married to Howard when reality hit me full force, like the collision that catapulted my father over the handlebars of the bike he was riding. Don't even ask why I thought it was reasonable for a 77 year old man who was a terrible driver in a car to steer a rented bike weaving around bikers and skaters along the crowded bike path on Venice Beach.

Fortunately he suffered no broken bones, just a badly split lip that was stitched up by a plastic surgeon later that day. It wasn't the injury itself that changed things, or got to me.

The sudden realization struck me harder than my dad hit the pavement: he was human, vulnerable. And he was getting older. At some point in the not too distant future, we would switch roles. He would no longer be capable of taking care of me and my brother and sister. Instead, we would take care of him, an unimaginable idea for someone whose entire life was about taking care of everyone else.

We called him The Patriarch, a title he loved. It fit him so well in life that we inscribed it on his gravestone after he died. I wish I had expressed my love and gratitude more often while Dad was here. But it's never too late for any of us to pay tribute and thank the ones we love, so here goes:

I don't appreciate inheriting the dark circles, but I have your eyes, and I know yours were always watching out for me.

I also don't appreciate inheriting the propensity for Alzheimer's, but I have your brain, and you taught me how to use mine.

You didn't show me your weaknesses, but I have your strength, that held me up and showed me I could hold myself up when you weren't there.

You always tried to protect me, but I have your resilience, which I learned by seeing you adapt every time you must have thought, *"I never signed up for this..."*

Dad had been gone more than a year when Carla asked me to come to Canyon Ranch to celebrate her 50th birthday. An outlier in a family of fitness fanatics, I don't get why a personal trainer whose daily life is about exercise would choose to do the same thing on her vacation. But I joined Carla and her husband Paul in Tucson, even though the bike ride up a mountain they scheduled for my first morning made me so sore I could barely move the rest of the trip.

So I was grateful for any breaks in the exercise classes. When I had first checked in, upon learning I was a cancer survivor, the resort advisor highly recommended a private session on the list of treatments, something called *Healing Touch*.

"Oh, they recommended that to us, too," Carla told me later. She and Paul had arrived at Canyon Ranch a few days before me. "We heard it was emotional, and life changing. So I did it before you got here. Total waste of time."

Even if she was right, it was an excuse to escape exercising. Healing touch was unlikely to make me sore, or even sweat. I showed up for my assigned appointment.

Sue Kagel came to get me from the waiting room and led me into a very small room at the end of the hall. I don't know what I was expecting, but I figured there would be some outward signs if healing touch was meant to inspire inward travel. The room had a leather-covered examining table like a massage table, but no incense, no candles burning, no inspiring art on the wall, nothing that hinted New Age.

As directed, I climbed onto the table and stretched out on my back, fully clothed. If nothing else I could shut my eyes and relax—which I did, while Sue asked a few questions about my history.

Briefly relating my story, I was struck by my long list of potential issues that needed healing. There were so many choices: six years after diagnosis, I was not on daily death watch but I was far from being in the clear with cancer. My scars had healed on the outside but not inside. I had not fully adjusted to my new body, missing both breasts and ovaries. My relationships needed healing, too. My marriage to V had survived some very shaky ground but it was still trembling. I still felt enormous guilt for causing pain to my children by moving them away from their father.

Sue told me very little about what to expect. What I remember is that she said she could not predict what might happen, but most likely, what might rise to the surface was what most needed healing.

I shut my eyes and tried to relax. I could sense rather than feel, her hands lightly passing over my body, not massaging, not pressing, not even really touching me. I lay there as I had so many sleepless nights, tormenting myself with my failures, my mistakes, my regrets, my wishes that I had done this instead of that, idly wondering what would rise to the top.

When it came, it didn't seem like something near the top, but from so deep inside me it felt like molten lava rushing to explode from a volcano. Tears gushed out like a great flood of biblical proportions. What I felt, what I sensed, what I KNEW was not something, but someone.

Years flew back in a breath. After I remarried and moved, dizzy in love, overwhelmed by the daily needs of two kids who missed their dad, I had not focused on how much I missed mine and how large that loss loomed over my life.

After my wedding to V, Dad continued coming out to California occasionally to see my kids when they were with Howard in Los Angeles. But he shut me out completely. I had heard stories of parents who sat shiva for children who married out of the Jewish faith. Though I don't know if Dad actually sat shiva, I was dead to him.

"Before I die, he'll have to speak to me," was one of my first and few positive thoughts on getting my cancer diagnosis.

Though I expected him to call as soon as he heard the news, our reconciliation came a few weeks later. We talked on the phone, a conversation that confounded me. Dad was the one and only person in the world I expected to feel the pain of my diagnosis as deeply as I did. But he didn't cry, didn't rant and rave, didn't apologize or agonize. I also assumed he would draw the line between the destinies of my mother and me, a line I had been tracing over and over in my mind. He never mentioned the link; didn't seem to connect the dots.

A few weeks later, he came to visit me in Carmel, staying in our home and meeting the man he had so opposed me marrying. For an occasion so weighted with emotion and drama, his visit was memorable for the lack of it. Cancer was a relatively minor part of the conversation; our shared history wasn't explored. An unfamiliar emptiness entered and seemed to reshape our relationship.

Self-involved and scared for myself, I didn't connect the dots either. Years later I understood it was not only the intellect but the emotions which are stolen by Alzheimer's, and Dad's emotional absence was a sign that he was in the early stages. We expected it; his mother had it, all three of her children would get it. In fact at the time he came to visit me, Dad was the main caregiver for his brother Phil, who was only one year older. Dad managed to mask his own limitations so well that none of us realized how far it had progressed until I visited him in Miami about a year after his visit to Carmel.

The first thing he said to me was, "You look thin." He's fine, I thought. This was classic Dad.

But an hour later, as I drove him to the cemetery to visit my mother's grave, he didn't remember how to get there. He seemed confused. "We're visiting Mom," I told him. "Marcella."

"Who's Marcella?" he asked me.

Alzheimer's denied me closure and a chance to bridge the distance with Dad. The emotional absence expanded. What my children remember about my dad is the man with vacant eyes who had no idea who we were. Though I knew it would not come, I longed for a sign of the man who had been my only parent, the patriarch who presided over our family. There was no shadow of that man in the shell of the one that remained, in whose eyes we could not find even a flicker of the father we knew.

And now I felt him in this room in Tucson, more than a year after his death which occurred on July 5, completing the cycle of devastating Independence Day weekends.

I squeezed my eyes shut tight, afraid if I opened them, I would lose him. My sobbing was so intense, I couldn't speak. Sue didn't speak either, but I could sense her encouragement to go with what was happening.

Not that I had any choice or control. Our relationship had been removed from my radar, but Dad was unquestionably present in that moment in that space: in my body, in my blood, in my soul, in that little room in Arizona. I felt him. I knew he was there. And I also knew why.

He wanted from me what I wanted from him, what life had not given us the chance to resolve. He was there to forgive, to forgive me and to allow me to forgive him

Yes, I forgive you, I told him silently through sobs. And yes, I know you forgive me.

I knew in that moment with every shred and fiber of my being that he was communicating with me, and I knew we were done. Resolved. In death we had closed the gap that separated us in life. All the dangling issues and unspoken words between us were washed away by the tears that would not stop.

And then I felt something else, not in the spiritual realm, but in the physical. Something pressing that was very much here in the present on earth.

"I have to pee," I told Sue, my eyes still shut. *Shit*, I thought, hating to interrupt my time with Dad.

"It's okay," she said, "just open your eyes and get up. The bathroom is down the hall to the right."

I got up, opened my eyes, and did what she told me, knowing in my heart that the spell would break, the moment would be lost. I walked down the hall, turned down another hall, and found the bathroom. Then I came back, past the waiting room where I had sat, past people in the hallways who had to be wondering why this woman was drenched in tears.

Back in the room with Sue, I climbed onto the table. "I know I'll never get it back. But I can't thank you enough for what you gave me. This was amazing."

Sue smiled. I shut my eyes again, and relaxed back into the table. Within two minutes I was again heaving gulping, gut-wrenching gobs of emotion. I can't recreate exactly what went on during the minutes I felt Dad. It was as if his spirit or soul was inside me, talking to me, and I could feel and hear exactly what he wanted me to know. And this time, after the peeing and after the forgiveness, what he wanted me to know was something I had always known and always felt but had never heard from him in my entire life. I heard it now: *I love you.*

Role Reversal

"It's not a big deal so don't overdo the drama." After two decades, knowing my tendencies toward anxiety, Howard downplayed the news that he had lymphoma, telling me over the phone, "It's very slow-growing and easy to treat. I don't even need chemo."

He minimized his situation so much that a few days later, when he was starting treatment, his longtime girlfriend wasn't planning to go with him to the doctor. I mentioned this to V, who happened to be down in Los Angeles on business.

"He shouldn't go alone. Having a support person on the scene makes a huge difference. You know what that's like," V told me.

I did. And knowing V, I knew exactly what would happen. The next morning Howard showed up at his oncologist's office, and found my husband waiting for him. V stayed with him all day for his first treatment.

It was the first infusion of many. Within a year what started as a mild form of lymphoma morphed into a more severe form. When it worsened, Howard decided to go for a consultation at MD Anderson Cancer Center in Houston. Again, he was planning to go alone.

Given my experience helping other cancer patients advocate for themselves, I insisted on being there. V encouraged me to go, and I met Howard in Houston. After several rounds of testing, we consulted with the doctor, who stunned us with the news that Howard's condition already was dangerously precarious. He processed paperwork on the spot, and Howard was admitted into the hospital immediately to begin chemo.

There's no place I've been that does a more stellar job at everything surrounding cancer than MD Anderson. Still, remembering how helpless I felt during my own cancer experience, at times I felt even more helpless being the caregiver for someone else. By now Howard had taken my guidance and become an unstoppable force, advocating for his own health. But I know it made a difference that I was there. No one should have to go through any part of cancer alone.

My two day trip lasted more than a week. Fortunately, Howard responded to the chemo and the immediate crisis was over. But not for long. A few months later, lymphoma came back. And it kept coming back, despite multiple courses of chemo, radiation, and a stem cell transplant. At that point, Howard heard from his doctors what every patient dreads: they had no more treatments to offer.

The guy who won every negotiation characteristically refused to give in. He found an alternative doctor. "Cure" is not a word I use carelessly, but that's the only way to describe what happened. Once Howard started on this alternative program, his lymphoma disappeared and didn't come back. Ever.

But the euphoria didn't last long. Lymphoma didn't recur, but Howard's previous treatment of chemotherapy and radiation caused him to develop Myelodysplastic Syndrome, known as MDS, a precursor to leukemia, which also damaged his chromosomes. There isn't much research or effective treatment for MDS, and although Howard pursued every possible option, it progressed within a couple years to a life-threatening situation. No one could have been more heroic or a more relentless fighter than Howard. But this was one battle he could not win.

Till Death Do Us Part

I drove home from Los Angeles, completely drained. Howard was gone, but he was everywhere around me. In my car, which he had helped me buy a few months earlier. On the road itself, the 300 miles between Los Angeles and Carmel that he had driven countless times over the years, coming up to visit our children.

I spent much of his last few months doing that same drive to help take care of him. Long after our divorce, even in the last stages of his illness, he would always call me when I was on the road, checking to see where I was. Then he would call right when he knew I'd be pulling up to my house in Carmel, making sure I arrived safely.

Here's a slightly altered version of what I said at the service after he died.

At the moment we said our vows I was crying, and I never actually said the words "I do." Howard always joked that our marriage wasn't officially legal. It sure was **binding**. *Even after our divorce, even after seventeen years of marriage to V, I'm standing here today.*

That is a testament to who Howard was.

When he died, a memory immediately popped into my mind. We were separated and I was still living in our house with the kids. After being gone almost a week on a business trip, I came home at night. A few minutes later, Howard brought the kids home. He had taken them to

Disneyland that day and they were both fast asleep in the car in their clothes. He carried them upstairs and put them in their beds, then went home to his apartment about fifteen minutes away.

A few hours later in the middle of the night, the house started shaking. It was the Northridge earthquake. Things were falling off the walls and shattering as I jumped out of bed and brought Alli and Daniel into my bed.

We had no power, no radio, no idea how much damage had been done.

I sat there in the bed with the two kids in the pitch black middle of the night, stunned and not sure what to do.

In a few minutes we heard the front door open. We saw a light and there was Howard with a flashlight, coming to take charge and take care of us.

That was January 17, 1994.

It was January 17 again, eighteen years later, when I stood there as Howard died. It felt like another earthquake.

I could not imagine my life or the world without Howard in it. I felt like I was sitting in the dark waiting for him to show up with the flashlight.

Along with his sense of humor, that defined him—always taking charge—and taking care of the people he loved.

This entire experience of cancer was his worst nightmare and also his finest hour. It showed Howard's character at its best. He'd always been resilient and relentless but now he was courageous and heroic. And still smiling.

That's the legacy he left all of us.

The greatest gift he gave our children was teaching them to do what he did that night eighteen years ago—to take charge.

And the greatest gift our children gave Howard was proving to him they could do that so he was able to leave, feeling at peace and secure that they could take care of themselves.

Howard loomed so large in my life, even several years after his death I still find it hard to imagine the world without him in it. As V says, Howard left a huge hole.

So here's ten things he'd want to know:

1. I miss you much more than I thought I would.

2. Since that last week of your life in the hospital, no one in the family has watched Fox News.

3. Though they lived with me, both of our kids are like you—really organized and frugal with money. I have no idea how that happened.

4. Your beloved Cubs extended their losing streak. Maybe you can put in a good word for them.

5. Although I'm married to V, sometimes I feel like a widow.

6. Even without your patronage, Costco has managed to stay in business.

7. Things happen all the time that only you would fully appreciate, and I constantly wish I could call you.

8. My phone still speed-dials you on its own. I don't have the heart to delete your name.

9. Your kids, family, and friends talk about you all the time with love, smiles, and funny stories.

10. After you died, the kids found the chocolate telegram in your freezer that you saved for thirty-five years. It's now in my freezer, and I promise to keep it for the next thirty-five years.

Putting the Fun in Funeral

Years ago, in the dark depths of Cancer World, I spent a lot of time thinking about death. This is a fairly routine side effect of cancer, and it takes varying forms. For people with religious convictions, it might mean thinking about Heaven or Hell, a stop at the pearly gates, meeting with God or a supreme being. For the deeply spiritual, it can mean plumbing the depths of one's heart, thinking about the meaning of life, what you have contributed, and perhaps the next life to come.

Then there are shallow people like me. For us, death is scary but we're spared the intensity of contemplating the true meaning of what it means to die. I wasn't having morbid images, or worrying about how it might feel at the end of life, or wondering whether I'd see a white light. Mostly I agonized over what it would be like for my children after I was gone.

This train of thought led just a little ways down the tracks to thinking about my funeral. My preoccupation grew pretty constant, and pretty involved, kind of like advance event planning. Where would it be? Who would be there? Who would come from out of town? Who would eulogize me? What would they say? Was it too soon to start planning it now?

I imagined what I wanted for my funeral with lots of details—music to be played, food to be served, and most of all, people from different times and places that were part of my life meeting each other, reminiscing, sharing memories.

192

The more I ran the video of my virtual funeral inside my brain, the more it struck me: My funeral was going to be a once-in-a-lifetime occasion, a great social event where I would know every single person in the room, and I was going to miss it.

Could life possibly be more unfair?

If you're an introvert, your funeral provides the ultimate excuse to skip a social gathering. But as a party animal, I didn't see the point of people coming from near and far when the person who would *most* appreciate that scenario would be in the coffin. This called for an out-of-the-box solution (painfully obvious pun intended.).

If I was going to die, I figured, I could have my funeral *beforehand.* I'd get to see all the people from my past and present who I would not see in the future. Not only would they suffer the standard guilt that makes us feel obligated to attend funerals, they would have the added burden that the soon-to-be-dearly-departed would know whether they'd bothered to come. Obviously, everyone would show up.

This dress rehearsal funeral concept seemed promising, although there were a few thorny issues. Like how far in advance should I have this event? And how would I be able to predict when to schedule it? If I waited till the very end, I would look and feel terrible—there's a reason they call it being at death's door. On the other hand, having my funeral prematurely could prove embarrassing, especially if I lived too long afterwards. Plus it also might be kind of a jinx.

Then again, wasn't death the ultimate excuse, granting freedom to chuck all the rules and do whatever I wanted? I was becoming more comfortable playing the cancer card when I needed to. People would just have to forgive me if I held my funeral at the wrong time.

I became more invested in this pseudo-funeral, and then it suddenly dawned on me: What if I lived? I hated to give up my plan. The funeral idea seemed like so much...fun.

So I made a deal with myself. I would have my event no matter what. If I was going to die, I'd figure out an appropriate time for my funeral bash ahead of the big day itself. If I made it to fifty, five years away and the first big milestone for a cancer survivor, I would throw myself a big birthday party. I got the party either way, live or die, so it was a win/win situation. Well, sort of.

I never was a big party giver or made much fuss over my own birthdays. That was about to change. After having cancer, unlike most women my age, having a birthday really made me happy. Joyous, even. Every time I turned a year older, more than anything else, it meant I was *still here*.

Considering my mother's history and my own, I never expected to reach fifty. So when I got there, I had the party I always wanted. I just hadn't known how much I had wanted it, and how much it would mean.

What a blessing to bring all the people from different parts of my life together. What an experience to see them meet and mingle. Friends got to know the friends I'd been telling stories about for years. After finally going through all the photos I had been throwing into unsorted boxes for decades, I displayed them on enormous posters labeled with captions, like giant collective scrapbooks of my life. Everyone in the entire room could find their own picture somewhere, and we also took a group photo that I gave out as party favors with personal messages I wrote ahead of time to each guest.

Since this event put a different spin on a funeral, it fit to have a reverse twist on a eulogy. It wasn't about me, it was about everyone else. I had a captive audience and the opportunity of a lifetime: the chance to tell each person individually and publicly how he or she had contributed to my life and how grateful I was to have each of them there. I explained the origin of the party, back when I was living in Cancer World and thinking about my death. And I made them all a promise: since they had come to my 50th birthday party, everyone present was officially off the hook and welcome to skip my funeral.

Happily Ever After

How do you follow a funeral? I was still very much alive when this question came up.

Closing in on ten years of survival after cancer, I couldn't allow that major milestone to pass without commemorating it in a meaningful way. But it could be tricky. And tacky. After all, most people only have *one* funeral. I had some grave doubts.

I also had to contend with fate and all the bad stuff swirling around Independence Day: my diagnosis, divorce, and the deaths of both parents. Typically I spent July 4 weekend homebound, hidden away and hunkered down to avoid anything bad happening: appendicitis, an accident, an aneurysm.

But this occasion definitely demanded attention, something more dramatic than dinner out with the family. So I took my cue from the date and the spirit of independence. Since those ten years had liberated me from many things, maybe my personal Doomsday could become another one. Survival presented the perfect opportunity to declare independence from negative karmic overload and reverse it by creating proactive, positive karma. (After more than thirty years here, writing that sentence proves I've truly become a Californian.)

I had an obvious date and an obvious theme. The signs from the universe pointed to a celebration. To hell with the weekend from hell.

The date, the theme, and the logo for my party.

For a party animal like me, there's no celebrating without people. So again I brought people together, especially those who had been important to my cancer journey.

No one had been more closely attached, and aligned with my post-cancer experience than Mark Renneker M.D. For almost the entire ten years as my most trusted medical advisor, he had intimate knowledge of my health and my strategy, guiding me every step along the way. On the night of my party, he was among those who chose to speak. In all the years he'd been practicing medicine, he told everyone, he'd attended many funerals. Yet in all that time, he said, mine was his first and only celebration party. From his perspective, more people could and should take the opportunity to celebrate.

I couldn't agree more, and I wish more survivors would mark what are sometimes called *cancerversaries* by celebrating in their own ways. Surviving cancer is an accomplishment.

Surviving any challenge is an accomplishment. Why not celebrate what you've survived—by doing whatever is meaningful to you?

Besides people, my celebration centered around *things* that were meaningful to my healing, kind of like a grownup version of *Show and Tell*. My breasts made a return appearance, even in

The boob at the bottom wasn't part of a set; when I wore it I still had the matching one.

absentia. Displayed on a table was my extensive collection of fake boobs I had worn in various sizes and shapes, including an exact replica made by a Hollywood special effects person of my cancerous breast that I had worn as a prosthetic. I encouraged everyone to think of this as a hands-on exhibit.

One popular party activity was a contest. Each table of guests competed as a team to list the most synonyms for *breasts*. Jugs, hooters, ta-tas, bazooms; the winning table came up with more than thirty words.

My celebration was an outward expression of my authentic self, how I had changed and grown, and who I had become. Part of it involved putting out what I had taken in, sharing what I had learned about resilience, about survival, about life.

One tangible way I did that was by sharing what art had meant in my journey. Besides displaying what I made myself, I shared the Glazes experience. Each guest got an apron, and a chance to sit at a table and paint tiles like I paint for my mosaics. Finally people could get what I had been talking about—my friends and family found the experience as relaxing and therapeutic as I did.

As reminders of my celebration, I gave out souvenirs, but I saved the best one for myself. After the party, I took all the tiles everyone had painted, put them together, and surrounded them with more broken pieces.

This table truly is one of my treasures. It makes me smile every single time I see it. It's more than a meaningful memory of people I love coming together to celebrate. It's a tangible reminder of what mosaics represent. Our resilience. Our ability to rebound from challenges. Our inner resources that allow us to survive and grow.

Since I made my table, ten more years have passed. Over that time, I've accumulated plenty more broken pieces. But I've also traveled to new places, started new ventures, seen my children grow up. And I've lived long enough to get my Medicare card!

So bring on the broken pieces. We each have the power to pick up those pieces, to rearrange them, to create something new, to be the artist of our own lives, every messy mysterious miraculous moment.

Appendix
My Survival Kit: The Top 10

Writing this book provided me with a window into my own journey, including an assessment of the most important tools that became components of my mental/emotional survival kit.

So I thought I would put together a Top Ten List, the tools that worked best for me. I can't say if all of them, or even any of them, will be on the list for anyone else. We develop our resilience and survival skills in our own unique ways, based on our own experiences, our own needs, our own strengths. What's important is not what's in your survival kit, but that you have one. Here's mine:

1. Laugh out loud and as often as possible.
Science has proven that humor is good for your health. If you *choose* to find the humor, you will. Even in the darkest moments, somewhere there is a laugh lurking, or at least a smile.

2. Don't be a victim.
Life is not fair, and you're not the only one who notices that. So shake off self-pity and siphon into your strength. Resilience is part of the DNA passed down from ancestors who survived. Somewhere, it's in you, too.

3. Keep your eyes and your mind open.
Life is full of surprises, good and bad. It doesn't unfold or look the way we expect. Our answers and angels don't always look like we expect, either.

4. Go with your gut.

No one knows what you need and want better than you. Learn how to tune in and figure out what your intuition and your instincts tell you, then learn to trust them.

5. Have a support system.

Hopefully you are lucky enough to be surrounded by supportive people. If the casseroles don't roll in, don't wait around for them. Ask for what you need and want. Having relationships is the best possible prescription for good health.

6. Ground yourself in gratitude.

Gifts can come from bad things, and there are gifts all around us. Learning to notice and appreciate them is one of the best gifts you can give yourself.

7. Seek perspective, not perfection.

Who has ever achieved perfection, anyway? Having perspective is the not-so-secret ingredient for satisfaction in life.

8. Live in the moment.

There's a reason almost every spiritual teacher reinforces this message. The present is all we really have. Don't let it go by without being there.

9. Find what nourishes you. Repeat as often as you can.

Music, meditation, macramé—find your own magic. Nourishment is not all about what you put into your body. It's just as important for the soul to soar.

10. Celebrate your survival and your successes.

Overcoming any challenge is an accomplishment. Yet what we admire or acknowledge in someone else, we might overlook in ourselves. You deserve to be honored and celebrated. So do it.

Acknowledgements

As a reader, I love reading acknowledgements, maybe because I always appreciate getting a peek behind the scenes. This book evolved out of my talk at TEDX Napa Valley, and the people who were part of that process also helped me birth this book (to use the most over-used analogy ever).

For years I've been straddling two worlds—online and off. Some people who were pivotal to this book, I've never met, although their support is very real. My gratitude to Karin Lippert for generosity; to Melissa Schultz, Lynne Spreen, Rachel Thompson, for steering me toward assistance; to Bridget Boland, Toni Rakestraw for editing; Rachel Resnick for helping me tap into my story; Elke Weiss for the cover and for truly being magic.

If I spent less time online, this book would have been published way sooner. So no thanks for distracting me, but many thanks for being there. That means you, friends on Facebook, Twitter, Instagram. That means you, blog readers who stuck around as my posts dwindled from once a day to once a semester. That means you, women of Midlife Boulevard, Flat and Fabulous, Creative Alliance, Behind the Pink Moon, and cancer survivors who inspire me every single day.

Thank you to the incredible team behind TEDx Napa Valley for fulfilling the first item on my bucket list before I had a bucket list. Thanks to Rebecca Costa, Paula Herman, Susan McBeth, Eileen McDargh, Larry Levy, Cindy Myers, Rob Berkley, Nicki Durlester for input and expertise. I'm thrilled that writing this book led me back to Sue Kagel, who led me to peace with my father. I'm honored to be connected in any way with Suzanne Braun Levine and Hope Edelman, who have inspired me for years. They are not only wonderful writers but wonderful human beings.

Shout out to the women of WHOA!, including my fabulous friend and partner Lynn Forbes; Shari Freedman who first planted the idea of a TED talk; Tracey Lally for the depth of her dedication.

Although some of my journey involved bucking the medical system, in no way does this imply a lack of admiration, respect, and enormous gratitude to anyone who played a role in my health care, either now or then. People who are involved in caring for cancer patients are all heroes in my book.

Every single day I think about how lucky I am to be surrounded and lifted up by wonderful friends. Some of them crossed over from personal to professional to support me during the course of this project. Deep gratitude to Myra Goodman for her genius, generosity and encouragement at crucial times…actually, at all times. Heartfelt appreciation to Deborah Rothschild for perspective in helping shape my thinking; Charlotte Brown for pointing her brilliance and humor in my direction; Sarah Browne, for sharing insight and information stored in her brain; Iris Dart, for valuable input and suggestions; Barbara Weller for creative thinking and ideas.

Thank you to friends whose stories I shared, and to those who know the stories behind the stories. I could not have written this book much less function without Jane Marcus, Laurie Benjamin, Judy Brooks, Arlyne Rothberg, Nancy Moonves, Deborah Rothman, the Beach Babes, Carol Levy, Marsha McMurrain, Josh Pollack, Carla and Paul Rosenthal.

Alli and Daniel are part of, and the heart of, everything I do. That includes this book, and one of my kids turned out to be an incredible editor. I'm not naming names but I can't help bragging about her.

My husband V is the *first* person I look to for assistance and advice; but he always jokes that he comes *last* on my list. So here is official proof that for once, he's right.

P.S. I might have just thanked every single person who is going to buy this book. Yet I'm still worried that maybe I forgot someone. So if you're reading this and you deserve acknowledgement, please accept my apologies and my promise that you'll be in the next book. And I hope you'll still read this one!

Made in the USA
San Bernardino, CA
09 October 2015